Sixth Edition

A Short History of the French Revolution

Jeremy D. Popkin

University of Kentucky

LONDON AND NEW YORK

First published 2015, 2010, 2006 by Pearson Education, Inc.

Published 2016 by Routledge
2 Park Square, Milton Park, Abingdon, Oxon OX14 4RN
711 Third Avenue, New York, NY, 10017, USA

Routledge is an imprint of the Taylor & Francis Group, an informa business

Library of Congress Cataloging-in-Publication Data

Popkin, Jeremy D.,
A short history of the French Revolution/Jeremy D. Popkin, University of Kentucky.—Sixth edition.
pages cm
Includes bibliographical references and index.
ISBN 978-0-205-96838-1 (alk. paper)—ISBN 0-205-96838-4 (alk. paper) 1. France—History—Revolution, 1789–1799. 2. France—History—Consulate and First Empire, 1799–1815. 3. Revolutions—History—19th century. I. Title.
DC148.P67 2015
944.04—dc23

2014022447

ISBN 13: 978-0-205-96845-9 (pbk)

CONTENTS

PREFACE

From the time that it took place down to our own day, the French Revolution has always been recognized as one of those occurrences that truly changed the world. When the French people in 1789 overthrew the monarchical system under which they had lived for centuries and replaced it with a written constitution that redefined their country's political system and social structure, they were trying to implement new ideas about government and society, ideas that have become the basis of life, not only in France, but also in much of the rest of the modern world. The dramatic struggles of the French Revolution provoked debates that are still relevant today. These debates raised questions about the nature of liberty and equality; the extent of human rights; the legitimate powers of government; the definition of nationhood; slavery and racial prejudice; the relations between the sexes; the legitimacy of political violence; and the ability of human beings to control their own destiny. The Revolution and the succeeding Napoleonic era saw the most extensive wars Europe had ever known and set the stage for the development of modern nation-states and ultimately for the conflicts and revolutions that have marked the history of the past two centuries.

Because of their importance, few historical events have been studied more closely than those that took place in France between 1789 and 1815. A vast literature seeks to explain the origins of the Revolution, the goals of its leaders, and the role of ordinary men and women in its events and to draw up the balance sheet of its successes and its failures. That literature continues to grow because historians continue to approach the Revolution with new questions in mind. Nineteenth-century scholars weighed the revolutionaries' contributions to the ideals of constitutional government and Napoleon's impact on the art of warfare. As modern working-class movements grew at the beginning of the twentieth century, historians focused on the importance of popular participation in the Revolution. The rise of Communist and Fascist totalitarianism directed attention to the workings of the Jacobin dictatorship and the Napoleonic regime. Current interests in the role of women in the past, the cultural dimension of history, the historical role of violence, and the interaction of European and non-Western peoples have directed attention to areas often ignored in earlier studies.

This short account attempts to introduce students to the major events that make up the story of the French Revolution and to the different ways in which historians have interpreted them. It makes no claim to be comprehensive: no single volume can hope to encompass all aspects of the revolutionary drama. This volume will have served its purpose if it succeeds in helping instructors share the excitement of studying this unique period of the past with their classes and if it encourages students to undertake further exploration of the subject.

New to This Edition

This new edition of *A Short History of the French Revolution* has been updated to reflect the latest scholarship on the subject, in fields ranging from women's history and the issue of political violence to the revolutionary struggles over race and slavery and relations between France and the United States.

Updates include:

- New coverage of women during the Revolution
- New coverage of the struggles over race and slavery
- New coverage of the relationship between France and the United States
- New coverage of political violence during the Revolution
- Expanded cultural coverage throughout
- Learning objectives provide pedagogical guidance on main themes of each section
- Further reading suggestions include publications on the Revolution and Napoleon through the end of 2013

Acknowledgments

I would like to thank the following reviewers for their insight and suggestions: Laura Mason, Johns Hopkins University; Jay Smith, University of North Carolina–Chapel Hill; Jack Censer, George Mason University; Paul Hanson, Butler University; Daniel Gordon, University of Massachusetts; Samuel Crompton, Holyoke Community College; Michael Dettelbach, Smith College; David Hunt, University of Massachusetts, Boston; Jill Harsin, Colgate University; the late Edgar Leon Newman, New Mexico State University; Dmitri Shlapentokh, Indiana University; Richard Bienvenu, University of Missouri; Tom Ewing, Virginia Tech; Gillian Glaes, Carroll College; and Joan Landes, Penn State.

CHAPTER 1

The Origins of the French Revolution

LEARNING OBJECTIVES

After studying this chapter, you will be able to:

- **Explain the difficulties facing the French absolute monarchy in the years preceding the French Revolution.**
- **Define the major groups making up French society and explain the reasons for their dissatisfaction with their situation.**
- **Discuss the major ideas of the Enlightenment and the changes in mentalities that took place in the last decades of the Old Regime.**

Late on the night of 14 July 1789, Louis XVI, king of France, met with the duke of La Rochefoucauld-Liancourt, one of his courtiers, to discuss the dramatic news he had just received. In the capital city of Paris, fifteen miles from his palace of Versailles, a crowd had stormed the royal fortress of the Bastille. "Is it a revolt?" the bewildered king supposedly asked, thinking that the event was no more than a directionless outbreak of violence that could quickly be brought under control. "No, Sire, it is a revolution," the duke is said to have replied.

For more than two centuries, historians all over the world have agreed with that assessment. The events of 14 July 1789 marked the overthrow of a centuries-old system of government and society, and the beginning of a new era for France and the entire Western world. The storming of the Bastille caught Louis XVI by surprise. Having spent his entire life in the closed world of his aristocratic court, he was largely unaware of the many tensions in France's institutions, its social order, and its culture. With the advantage of hindsight, however, historians can identify the fault lines that made a revolution possible, if not inevitable.

The Problems of the Monarchy

After the French Revolution started, supporters frequently offered a very simple explanation of its cause. They had risen up, they said, against a system of tyranny or despotism, in which all power was monopolized by a single man, the king, and by his arbitrarily chosen ministers.

As an example of this excessive power, they could cite the words of Louis XV, who told some recalcitrant magistrates in 1766 that according to French law, "the sovereign power resides in my person only."[1] This was not mere rhetoric: critics of absolutism could also cite real examples of the king's arbitrary and unrestrained power, such as his ability to issue *lettres de cachet,* arrest warrants that allowed the imprisonment of any subject without a trial (see Document A).

In reality, this characterization of the Old Regime monarchy as despotic is greatly exaggerated. Prerevolutionary France was indeed an absolute monarchy—that is, one in which all sovereign powers, including the right to make laws and to enforce them, the right to appoint judges and officials, and the right to make war and to sign treaties were exercised exclusively by the king. But the French legal theorists who had developed the principles of royal absolutism from the late sixteenth century onward had always insisted that the king's absolute powers were neither arbitrary nor tyrannical. The king was obligated to rule according to laws and customs that had accumulated over the ages. He could not, for example, alter the rules of hereditary succession, which dictated that the throne passed to his closest living male relative. Indeed, in explaining the political difficulties that led to the Revolution of 1789, modern historians are more likely to stress the weaknesses of the monarchy rather than its excessive concentration of power.

The weakness that was most responsible for precipitating the Revolution was the government's inability to balance its income and its expenses. Laws and customs required the French monarchy to fulfill many costly responsibilities; they also limited the king's ability to raise money to pay for these obligations. The king's

DOCUMENT A

Louis XV States the Principles of Absolutism

On 3 March 1766, after repeated quarrels with the judges of the Paris Parlement, who insisted on their right to object to royal decrees, Louis XV convened a lit de justice, a ceremony used to compel the magistrates to accept the royal will. He seized the occasion to remind the judges of the principles of French absolutism, as they had developed by his predecessor Louis XIV.

"It is in my person alone that the sovereign power resides, whose special character is the spirit of prudence, of justice, and of reason... I alone exercise the power of making laws, independently and undividedly...the entire public order proceeds from me and the rights and interests of the nation, which some have dared to separate from the monarch, are necessarily united with mine and rest exclusively in my hands."

(Translation by Jeremy D. Popkin.)

CORONATION OF LOUIS XVI

The traditional symbols that dominate this announcement of Louis XVI's coronation in 1775 give no hint of the modern ideas that affected even the ruler and his advisors. The king takes his crown from a saint holding the cross, indicating the divine origins of his powers, while angels behind him carry banners and emblems associated with the French monarchy since the Middle Ages.

duty to maintain domestic order required keeping up police forces and guards scattered throughout territories that made up the largest kingdom in western Europe, as well as judges, courts, and prisons. External defense was even costlier. Like all other European monarchs, the king of France governed a state in constant rivalry with its neighbors. Kings were taught from birth that they must defend the lands they inherited but also that they should seek opportunities to extend them, thereby acquiring the glory that was an essential element of kingship.

Through a long series of conquests and acquisitions, the kingdom of France had grown from a medieval principality centered around the capital city of Paris into the largest and most populous state in Europe, with around 28 million inhabitants in 1789; about a million more people, mostly black slaves, lived in France's overseas colonies. The kings of the Bourbon dynasty, the ancestors of Louis XVI, ruler at the time of the Revolution, had all engaged in warfare to enlarge their realm. They had built up a kingdom that extended from the lowlands of Flanders in the north to the Pyrenees and the Mediterranean Sea in the south, from the Atlantic Ocean in the west to the Rhine River and the Alps in the east, and that included colonies in Canada, the Caribbean, and the Indian subcontinent. To do so, they had built up a costly military machine. Under Louis XIV, king from 1643 to 1715, the French army had grown to 400,000 men, the largest Europe had ever seen, and made other rulers fear that France aimed to dominate the entire continent. Louis XV and Louis XVI were less aggressive, but they nonetheless felt a responsibility to keep France strong and to protect its interests and its reputation abroad.

Some of the problems that led to the French Revolution stemmed from costly efforts to maintain France's position relative to the other European states and especially from its rivalry with the British. Britain, a naval power with a fast-growing economy, was able to concentrate on building up its colonial empire, while France also had to contend with rivals on the continent, particularly Austria and Prussia. The country's poor performance in the eighteenth century's most extensive conflict, the Seven Years' War (1756–1763), raised fears that the French monarchy was unable to cope with these challenges. While Prussian king Frederic the Great, a brilliant commander, inflicted humiliating defeats on French armies in Europe, the British used their control of the seas to capture French colonial possessions in India and North America. Two years before Louis XV's death in 1774, France stood by helplessly as Prussia, Austria, and Russia annexed territories belonging to Poland, one of its traditional allies.

Early in Louis XVI's reign, France rebounded from these foreign policy defeats by aiding Britain's American colonies in their war for independence. French troops and the French fleet significantly aided the Americans, and France hosted the peace conference at which England conceded the colonies' independence in 1783. However, this success cost France a great deal of money and brought none of the tangible rewards in the form of new territories that usually marked a victory. Fear of adding even more debt kept France from aiding its Dutch allies when Prussia intervened in the Netherlands in 1787. French public opinion blamed the monarchy for allowing a smaller power to humiliate it.

In addition to maintaining his power and glory, the French king was expected to see to the welfare of his subjects. The king maintained the country's main roads.

His courts provided justice for his subjects. In times of crop failure, royal officials in the provinces were expected to organize relief. Through its expanding system of royal academies, the government subsidized writers, artists, scientists, doctors, and even veterinarians; starting in the 1760s, the king funded training for midwives, in an effort to reduce rates of maternal and infant mortality. The most visible royal expense, the upkeep of the court at the palace of Versailles, accounted for only a small percentage of the monarchy's spending, but it was a symbol of extravagance that made it difficult to win support for reforms meant to enable the monarchy to meet its other obligations.

To carry out all these responsibilities, the royal government had developed an extensive administrative network. Louis XIV, the most strong-willed and efficient of the Bourbon kings, had established a system of *intendants*, appointed royal officials stationed in each of the country's provinces and responsible for carrying out royal orders. Subordinate officials extended the intendants' reach to smaller towns and villages. France's system of administration was considerably more centralized than that of most other European states; in theory, royal power could be exerted everywhere in the kingdom.

In practice, however, this centralized administration ran into many obstacles. Each province, each region, each town had its own special laws and institutions, which the intendant could not simply ignore. From the humblest peasant to the haughtiest noble, the king's subjects were imbued with the notion that they had rights and privileges that they were entitled to defend. This legalistic outlook was reinforced by the conduct of the royal appeals courts, the thirteen *parlements,* whose judges, all members of the nobility, claimed the right to review all royal laws and edicts to ensure that they were in conformity with the traditional laws of the realm.

Although the parlements were royal courts, the king's influence over the judges was limited because they literally owned their court seats. The sale of government posts was one of the ways in which the French monarchy made up for its inadequate sources of revenue. Posts purchased this way became family property that could be passed down to heirs, regardless of their qualifications, or sold for a profit. These posts were desirable because offices conferred social prestige and, in many cases, granted their holders noble status. But this system of venal office-holding greatly reduced the efficiency of the royal administration. Venal office-holders often used their positions to benefit themselves and their families rather than to carry out their duties.

The parlements claimed that it was their duty to resist actions that violated the traditional laws of the kingdom and the rights of the king's subjects, such as efforts to raise taxes. In the absence of institutions of representative government, the parlements claimed to defend the interests of the "nation" against arbitrary authority. In practice, the parlements' objections often amounted to a defense of privileged groups' special interests, including those of the judges. But the parlements' denunciations of arbitrary rule and their insistence that the "nation" had a right to participate in political decision-making spread ideas about representative government among the population. Paradoxically, the privileged noble judges of these royal courts were forerunners of a revolution that was to sweep away all special privileges.

The Failure of Reform

Throughout the second half of the eighteenth century, royal ministers recognized that the French government needed more revenue if it was going to maintain its international standing and meet its domestic obligations. But the problem of raising taxes illustrated better than anything else the institutional problems facing the monarchy. In theory, the king should not have had much trouble raising more money. Unlike the king of Great Britain, France's ruler had no need to negotiate with a representative body or parliament before he collected and spent money. The size of the kingdom and its rulers' need for a large army to defend it from foes who, unlike those of Britain, could easily threaten its borders had limited the role of the assembly of the Estates-General—France's equivalent to the British Parliament—and finally enabled kings to stop convening it altogether after 1614. They had established their right to collect traditional taxes without going through any legislative process. But this authority came at a price: unlike the king of England, the French ruler lacked any regular mechanism for negotiating an increase in revenue as the kingdom's needs grew. He could collect only those taxes that had become customary over the years, and many subjects were able to evade payments because of equally customary exemptions.

A cumbersome and inefficient system of tax collection was another handicap for the prerevolutionary monarchy. Different provinces and different groups of subjects all paid different taxes. Rather than employing tax collectors who worked directly for the king, the government leased out the collection of most taxes to wealthy entrepreneurs, called tax farmers, who paid the treasury a set fee in exchange for the right to collect taxes in a given region. This system provided the monarchy with a dependable flow of income, but it also gave the tax farmers the incentive to squeeze as much as they could from the population, while forwarding as little as possible to Versailles. The tax farmers were also responsible for enforcing the government's unpopular monopoly on the sale of tobacco; their armed guards engaged in frequent confrontations with smugglers who often had the population's support because they sold the product at lower prices. The multiplicity of taxes and tax-collection enterprises made rational management of the royal income nearly impossible.

The last decades of the monarchy witnessed repeated efforts to rationalize and increase taxes and to make the French economy more productive, so that the government could extract more money from its subjects. In the 1760s, the government, urged on by a group of economic reformers known as the Physiocrats who preached the virtues of free trade, abolished traditional restrictions on grain sales, hoping to encourage production and thereby to expand the tax base. These plans broke down when bad harvests produced shortages that led to popular protests. In 1770, Louis XV appointed a strong-minded set of ministers who made a more determined effort to overcome the obstacles that were frustrating reform. The justice minister Maupeou ousted the obstructionist judges of the parlements, replacing them with more pliable appointees, while the finance minister Terray tried to write off much of the royal debt.

Maupeou's attack on the parlements was widely denounced as a "coup," and when Louis XV died unexpectedly in 1774, his inexperienced successor, Louis XVI, was persuaded to dismiss the controversial ministers and abandon their policies. The new ministers he appointed made their own efforts at reform, however. In 1776, Turgot, the controller-general, tried to revamp the organization of France's economy even more extensively than his predecessors in the 1760s. In accordance with Physiocratic principles, Turgot not only lifted restrictions on the grain trade but also tried to abolish the urban guilds, whose regulations restricted competition in the production and sale of many manufactured goods. A wave of riots against high grain prices, resistance from guild members, resistance from women who objected to the merger of guilds reserved for them with organizations dominated by men, and opposition from the parlements defeated him. Turgot's more cautious successor, Necker, tried to save money by eliminating unnecessary offices and collecting taxes more efficiently. In 1781, he caused a sensation by publishing a summary of the government's income and expenses, giving the public an unprecedented look at the monarchy's financial condition.

Government reform efforts were not limited to fiscal matters. In the last decades before the Revolution, the monarchy took a number of measures that foreshadowed the more sweeping changes that followed 1789. It asserted its power to regulate the Church by suppressing some of the many convents and monasteries inherited from the past. New ideas about human rights were reflected in the abolition of torture in judicial cases. In the late 1770s, the minister Necker introduced representative assemblies in several provinces, trying to give public opinion some voice in lawmaking and administration. The country's Protestant minority, officially outlawed under Louis XIV, received basic civil rights in 1787, and edicts meant to limit the harsh treatment of slaves were issued in 1784 and 1785.

The fact that royal ministers undertook so many reform efforts shows that they were well aware of the problems undermining the French monarchy and of the new ways of thinking that were spreading in French society. The result demonstrated the accuracy of the celebrated nineteenth-century French historian Alexis de Tocqueville's comment that "the most perilous moment for a bad government is one when it seeks to mend its ways."[2] To justify their reform proposals, the royal ministers themselves criticized long-established customs and institutions, thereby undermining the legitimacy of the existing order. Those adversely affected by proposed reforms defended themselves by challenging the government's right to arbitrarily change time-honored institutions. The problems that provoked the French Revolution were thus not simply due to an outdated and inefficient structure of government. They were also rooted in France's complex, hierarchical social structure.

Social Structure and Social Crisis

French society before 1789 was largely structured on the principle of corporate privilege. The French king's subjects were all members of social groups—*corps,* or collective bodies—that claimed special rights setting them apart from others. Like the institutions of the monarchy, this social order had a long history. Medieval thought had divided society into three orders, or estates—clergy who prayed, nobles who fought, and peasants who farmed—each with its own special rights and responsibilities. Originally, for example, nobles did not pay taxes to the king, as peasants did, since they served him personally by fighting in his wars. Over the centuries, privilege had become much more complicated than this simple threefold division. New groups had appeared, such as the populations of France's towns, who received grants of special privileges, including certain tax exemptions. Within the towns, members of particular trades were organized into guilds, with the right to monopolize certain kinds of work and to set prices and wages. As the kingdom acquired new provinces, different regions came to have differing privileges, too. New provinces might maintain their own customary laws and special institutions, such as provincial estates, and they were often exempted from certain taxes. For example, Brittany, permanently joined to the kingdom only in 1532, did not pay the unpopular salt tax, the *gabelle*.

Almost every group in eighteenth-century France could claim some sort of special privilege, but the most visible privileged groups were the estates or orders of the Catholic clergy and the nobility. Because of their special status as mediators between God and humanity, members of the clergy enjoyed exemption from most taxes. They were subject only to their own Church court system. The Church had the right to collect its own tax, the tithe, from the laity. The Church as a whole was a wealthy institution: over the centuries, the donations of the faithful had given it extensive property scattered throughout the kingdom, amounting to 10 percent or more of the country's real estate. But income within the Church was very unevenly distributed. Bishops and the abbots and abbesses of wealthy monasteries and convents, normally members of noble families, lived in high style, but many parish clergy were much poorer. Critics both inside and outside the Church complained that the institution's wealth and privileges did little to promote the charitable and spiritual missions the clergy were supposed to fulfill.

Even more severe was the criticism of the privileges held by the titled nobility. The nobility had long since ceased to be a closed caste descended from medieval warriors. France's kings had promoted access to this privileged group by allowing descendants of numerous families that had enriched themselves through trade to obtain noble status by buying venal offices in the royal bureaucracy. Noble status was worth pursuing because it brought with it many privileges. The most visible of these was exemption from many of the most onerous taxes, particularly the *taille*, the main tax on the peasantry. By custom or by law, most top positions in the royal bureaucracy, the army, and the Church were reserved for nobles. Nobles were entitled to special seating in their parish churches; they were allowed to keep doves and rabbits, despite the damage these animals often did to farm crops; and the fact that only nobles could carry swords and put weathervanes on their houses made their special status particularly visible.

Most noble families owned at least some land, but there was an enormous difference between the small elite of aristocratic courtiers, whose landholdings were often spread across several provinces and who monopolized the most lucrative posts at court and in the Church, and the hundreds of rural gentry whose income was sometimes no more than that of a well-to-do peasant. Wealthier aristocrats were able to share the profits from large-scale commerce by investing in enterprises owned by commoners, thereby acquiring economic interests no different from those of their partners. Their poorer cousins, however, were often driven to fight to maintain the distinction between themselves and the rest of the population. The 1781 Ségur edict, which required army officers to prove four generations of noble descent, was a typical measure meant to reserve jobs for descendants of noble families that had no other resources to pass along to their children. Nobles recognized that any significant changes in France's political and social institutions would probably reduce their privileges. Some influential aristocrats accepted reform, assuming that they would still be regarded as the natural leaders of society, but most nobles saw such proposals as a threat to their positions and openly opposed them.

Many nobles and clergy also had rights as *seigneurs* (overlords) that affected the peasants who lived near their estates and even local townspeople. These seigneurial rights were attached to landed property, not to nobility per se, and by the eighteenth century, many wealthy non-nobles had purchased estates that included such rights. Seigneurial rights included the privilege of maintaining a court to settle local disputes, the right to collect various dues from local peasants, and sometimes the right to charge tolls on roads or bridges and to compel the local population to use the seigneur's grain mill or baking oven. These seigneurial dues and monopolies caused frequent disputes between their holders and the rest of the population. In the debates of the period, objections to noble privileges and to seigneurial rights were often mixed together: both appeared to perpetuate distinctions that served no valid purpose.

The clergy and the nobility in eighteenth-century France were the most visible groups with special privileges. But many other social groups in prerevolutionary France also possessed jealously guarded rights. Townspeople were exempt from the taille, the burdensome land tax, and from many other obligations that weighed on the rural population, though they paid a much-resented tax on food and wine. Journeymen workers and ambitious entrepreneurs chafed at the privileges of the guild masters. Most privilege-holding groups enjoyed benefits that made them better off than the others, but some groups lived under special restrictions. In 1685, Louis XIV had attempted to stamp out France's Protestant minority by revoking their special charter of privileges, the edict of Nantes. In 1787, Louis XVI granted some civil rights to the Protestants, who had kept up a semiclandestine existence throughout the century, but they still faced many legal restrictions. So did the small Jewish population, which included a wealthy community of Sephardim—descendants of Jews expelled from Spain and Portugal centuries earlier—in the southwest of France and a poorer but more numerous group of Ashkenazi (German) Jews in the northeastern province of Alsace. In the colonies, the *Code noir*, whose earliest version dated back to 1685, regulated the treatment of slaves. In theory, the law required masters to provide slaves with adequate food and clothing and limited the harshest punishments, although in practice these provisions were widely ignored. A 1777 edict, the *police des noirs,* imposed a special registration system on blacks who in metropolitan France. Any systematic reform of the system of corporate privileges would inevitably raise the question of the status of these groups.

The Third Estate

The many reform plans proposed in the decades before the Revolution paid special attention to the privileges of wealthy elites such as the clergy and the nobility, because their tax exemptions made them obvious targets of any scheme for increasing government revenue. The reforming ministers of the eighteenth century recognized that it would be difficult to levy more taxes on the poorer and less-privileged sectors of the population. On the other hand, the support of this "Third Estate" might be enlisted in favor of reforms aimed at reducing the privileges of the First and Second Estates of the realm (the clergy and the nobility).

Members of the two privileged estates at least had their special privileges in common; the members of the Third Estate lacked any real unity. The Third Estate, which made up 97 percent of the population, included all the kingdom's commoners, from wealthy Parisian bankers who mixed easily with nobles to beggars who trudged the highways in search of food and work. Social historians use the term *bourgeoisie* to classify the richest stratum of the Third Estate: bankers, merchants, manufacturers, lawyers, and other educated professionals, as well as their wives and children. In the course of the eighteenth century, these groups profited from France's steady economic expansion. The period saw an especially significant growth in overseas trade. Merchants in seaports like Bordeaux, Nantes, and Marseille enriched themselves by exporting textiles, wines and liqueurs, and other French products and by investing in the slave trade that provided the labor force for the West Indian plantations from which France received sugar, coffee, indigo, and other tropical products. Manufacturers thrived on a growing domestic consumer market, as even the lower classes became able to purchase a wider variety of cheaper products and small luxuries.

Confident that they owed their success in life to their own efforts to obtain wealth and education, members of the bourgeoisie were often critical of nobles' special privileges. They also challenged the teachings of a Church that condemned the pursuit of worldly goods and routine business practices such as lending money at interest. Members of this growing bourgeois group were to be especially prominent in the revolutionary movement that developed in 1789, so much so that historians from the time of the Revolution to our own day have often explained that movement as a "bourgeois revolution." According to this thesis, first advanced by some of the revolutionaries themselves and most extensively elaborated by historians inspired by the nineteenth-century socialist theorist Karl Marx, the explosion of 1789 was the inevitable result of a system in which economic expansion swelled the ranks of the bourgeoisie, even as the workings of the system of privilege excluded them from social and political power.

Much recent historical research has undermined this explanation of the Revolution by emphasizing the degree to which the bourgeoisie at the end of the Old Regime shared common interests with many of the nobility, as well as the lack of unity among bourgeois groups. Nobles and bourgeois shared characteristics that set them apart from the remaining 90 percent of the French population. They were wealthy enough to be free of daily worries about subsistence, and they were educated—in fact, literacy levels were usually higher among the bourgeoisie than among the nobility. The frontier between the two groups was not closed. Throughout the eighteenth century, successful bourgeois families migrated into the ranks of the nobility, often investing the profits from their businesses in the purchase of landed estates. The two groups rubbed shoulders at the theater and in the Masonic lodges that were becoming increasingly popular as the end of the century neared. In many respects, the nobility and the bourgeoisie seemed to be merging to create a single elite, separated from the bulk of the population by its wealth and lifestyle. On the other hand, educated bourgeois lawyers and those wealthy enough to live off their investments had little in common with hardworking merchants focused on making money. The Revolution was to show, however, that the boundary between nobles and bourgeois remained significant enough so that, in certain circumstances, the members of the bourgeoisie could be led to unite and turn against the nobles. Although some prosperous bourgeois families could work their way up to noble status, the process remained slow and uncertain. The practice of reserving seats for nobles in the royal academies, which were supposed to reward outstanding merit, was one example of the practices that irritated members of the bourgeoisie.

Members of the bourgeoisie also had grievances against the French government. Bourgeois lawyers' interests were closely tied to the parlements. They shared the judges' conviction that France ought to be governed by regular laws, not by arbitrary royal enactments. Bourgeois families that had pinned their hopes for advancement on investment in government offices and that had put their savings into government bonds wanted to be sure that their positions would be protected. Merchants and manufacturers suffered in the uncertain economic climate of the 1770s and 1780s, as consumer demand stagnated and reform efforts like Turgot's abolition of the guilds were proposed and then revoked. Hopes that the newly independent American states would become a good market for French goods failed to materialize after the peace treaty of 1783, and French merchants complained when the government allowed the Americans to trade with the Caribbean colonies in 1784. The government stirred up a larger wave of protest from manufacturers in 1786 when it negotiated a free-trade treaty with Britain that exposed many French enterprises to stiff competition. When the revolutionary crisis began, many members of the bourgeoisie were receptive to the idea that they would benefit from social and political changes.

The Lower Classes

The power of the revolutionary movement that began in 1789 came from the fact that it mobilized not only the wealthy members of the bourgeoisie, but the far more numerous ranks of the urban and rural population. The more prosperous and more educated members of the bourgeoisie shared the lifestyle of the nobility; their poorer bourgeois cousins were not always sharply distinguished from the lower levels of the urban population. Many a merchant or manufacturer had started out as a shopkeeper or a hardworking artisan. Generally literate and relatively prosperous, these petty bourgeois heads of small family enterprises often exercised a strong social influence over the poorer and less-settled members of the urban population, those the upper classes referred to contemptuously as the *peuple,* the common people.

The memoirs of the Parisian glass-fitter Jacques-Louis Ménétra give us a rare firsthand glimpse into the life of a member of this stratum of French society. Like many skilled artisans, Ménétra went into his father's trade. He had the opportunity to spend several years making his *tour de France,* going from town to town to acquire training and experience. His adventures gave him a sense of independence, but his membership in a journeymen's organization, or *compagnonnage,* which defended workers' privileges, also taught him effective methods of collective action. Ménétra's memoirs show that he was familiar with some of the enlightened ideas that circulated among the bourgeoisie, particularly those critical of the Church. In his manuscript he wrote, "Is it possible that some men lord it over others by making them believe in chimeras and that we're dumb enough to believe in all their talk?"[3] Even before the Revolution, men like Ménétra had a sense that they could think and speak for themselves. His notion of independence had a strong masculine bias, however: he treated the women he met as fair game, although once he was married, he accepted the traditional arrangement that gave his wife control over the family money.

Guild masters' sons like Ménétra were better off than the majority of the urban working population. Most journeymen had little prospect of ever becoming owners of their own shops. They floated from job to job, always at risk of sinking into the ranks of unskilled day laborers or of falling ill and ending their days begging or dying in a hospice. Women, who made up a large part of the urban working population, had even less chance to achieve a privileged position. Turgot's reforms had abolished the all-women's guilds that had existed for occupations such as dressmaking. The wives of shop owners and guild masters worked alongside their husbands, often managing the family enterprise's money while their husbands did the physical work. Less fortunate women did low-paid piecework for entrepreneurs trying to get around guild regulations and make goods more cheaply. Women of the popular classes also often worked outside the home, as street vendors, laundresses, and seamstresses. Poor single women often worked as domestic servants, a position that put them in contact with members of the wealthier classes but that exposed them to dangers such as sexual exploitation that might in the end force them onto the streets as prostitutes.

Throughout the eighteenth century, the government had regarded the urban lower classes as a potential source of danger. Even though living standards for most had slowly improved over the course of the century, the ordinary people of the cities had simmering resentments against the wealthy and against a government that taxed their food and drink heavily but often seemed indifferent to their needs. Conflicts between employers and their workers were a regular occurrence. Popular protest often had a political impact as well. In 1775, a wave of riots against high prices defeated minister Turgot's effort to free the grain trade, and in 1786, silk weavers and other workers in Lyon, France's second-largest city, staged an insurrection that took three days to put down. The metropolis of Paris, whose population of nearly 600,000 made it far larger than any other city in France, was a particular concern. Even the poorer inhabitants of the capital were more educated and more aware of public events than their counterparts elsewhere. The Revolution would demonstrate how much impact they could have when they were aroused.

Much of the urban population consisted of migrants from the thousands of rural villages in which some three-fourths of the French population lived. Most peasants were poor by the standards of city dwellers, but conditions varied considerably from region to region, and within each village there were prosperous and impoverished families. Even observers of the time had contradictory impressions of the state of the peasantry. The English agricultural expert Arthur Young described Brittany as backward and poverty-stricken, with "husbandry not much further advanced, at least in skill, than among the Hurons," but at about the same time, another English traveler visited French Flanders and reported that "the most striking character of the country through which we passed is its astonishing fertility."[4]

Unlike the enserfed peasants of central and eastern Europe, the majority of French peasants had gained their legal freedom in earlier centuries. Just as the urban working classes ranged from prosperous skilled artisans to day laborers, prostitutes, and criminals living on the margin of subsistence, so these rural peasants varied from well-to-do *laboureurs* who contracted to manage wealthy seigneurs' estates to impoverished migrants who lived by taking odd jobs wherever they could find them. Most peasants owned some land, but only a minority had enough property to make their families economically self-sufficient. To make additional income, all members of peasant families, including women and children from an early age, had to contribute. Peasants hired themselves out to work on noble estates, rented land, or entered into sharecropping arrangements with local landowners. Many peasants also supplemented their income through cottage industries, such as spinning and weaving, which brought them into regular contact with bourgeois merchants. Peasants' social conditions also varied tremendously from region to region. In France's "breadbasket," the rich grain-growing region around Paris, a market-oriented, competitive economy split the peasants into a small elite of *coqs du village,* closely linked to the big landlords whose estates they managed, and a mass of poor peasants, forced to compete for jobs as laborers to supplement what they could raise on the tiny plots of property they owned. In the western provinces, less-developed economically, the income differences between peasant families were not as extreme, and the sense of tension between peasants and seigneurs less acute. These differences in rural social structure often influenced peasant reactions to the Revolution. Levels of education and literacy were usually lower in the countryside than in the towns, but some peasants could read and write. Thanks to the village priest, visitors such as traveling peddlers, and their contacts with nearby market towns, peasants had at least some sense of what was happening in the wider world. Parish assemblies gave villagers some experience in self-government even before the Revolution.

The slaves in France's overseas colonies lived far harder lives than the peasants. Captured in Africa and shipped across the Atlantic under horrifying conditions, they were put to work on sugar and coffee plantations, overseen by slave drivers who used the whip freely to enforce discipline. On the average, slaves brought from Africa only survived for seven to ten years, and the birth rate among them was too low to maintain their numbers. The years after the end of the American War were the height of the French slave trade, with more than 30,000 new slaves being imported annually to Saint-Domingue alone. Although plantation owners were confident that they could control the slaves through the use of terror, many of the new arrivals in the 1780s had fought in wars in Africa. Events after 1789 would show their ability to use military skills to fight for their freedom.

Although rural conditions differed considerably from region to region, unfavorable economic trends in the last decades before the Revolution also made the peasantry more restive. The reign of Louis XV, from 1715 to 1774, had been a prosperous one for most of the rural population. Crop failures had been rare, and the result had been a marked rise in population. Around 1770, however, climatic conditions took a turn for the worse, and in the two decades before 1789, economic hardship repeatedly struck the countryside. In years when bread prices rose sharply, peasants and the urban poor blamed efforts to create a free market in grain and called for government regulation. Even in calmer times, the growth in population increased the numbers of peasants competing for the available land and jobs, a situation that drove landlords' rents and food prices up but kept wages down. The growing split between rich and poor generated increased social tension. So did changing mentalities. As more secular attitudes penetrated the countryside, peasants became less tolerant of inequitable social arrangements. As events in 1789 were to show, under the right circumstances, the peasants could become a powerful revolutionary force.

New Ideas and New Ways of Living

Just as explanations of the French Revolution that emphasize social tensions were first advanced by the movement's supporters at the time, explanations stressing the influence of radical ideas go back to the movement's early critics, such as the British writer Edmund Burke. Burke and other opponents of the Revolution frequently blamed it on the baleful influence of the major French thinkers of the eighteenth century, the *philosophes,* whose criticism of established institutions had supposedly paved the way for the crisis of 1789. Over the past two centuries, historians have continued to debate the role of ideas in bringing about the Revolution. Modern scholars are less likely to attribute responsibility to specific writers, ideas, and books. More often, they emphasize the importance of new habits of mind and behavior, many of them fostered not by radical critics of society but by the workings of Old Regime institutions themselves or by gradual changes in everyday life.

It is certainly true that eighteenth-century French thinkers often criticized their country's leading institutions. The philosophes, the leading representatives of this movement of the Age of Enlightenment, applied to religious and social issues the rational approach to the world developed by scientists studying the natural world in the seventeenth century. As early as 1721, the baron de Montesquieu's youthful satire, *The Persian Letters,* mocked Catholicism and Louis XIV's absolutist government. In his masterwork, *The Spirit of the Laws,* first published in 1748, Montesquieu argued that there was no single legitimate political system. His positive portrayal of England's constitutional monarchy, which divided power between the king and the Parliament, was an implicit criticism of the French system, which Montesquieu claimed was kept from becoming despotic only by the activity of beleaguered "intermediate bodies" such as the parlements. Throughout the rest of the century, critics of absolutism repeated Montesquieu's ideas and spread the notion that France needed independent institutions capable of limiting the power of the king and his ministers.

The poet, playwright, and pamphleteer Voltaire was another of the most influential philosophes. He aimed his sharpest barbs at religious orthodoxy. His popular plays like *Mahomet,* which was based on the life of the founder of Islam, castigated religious intolerance and fanaticism; his short novels, such as *Candide* and *Zadig,* raised troubling questions about whether God truly provided humanity with clear rules to live by. Voltaire gained particular fame near the end of his life, in the 1760s, when he devoted himself to winning justice for several victims of religious persecution in France, particularly the Protestant Jean Calas, unjustly executed on charges of having murdered a son who converted to Catholicism. Although he denounced injustice and intolerance and helped popularize the notion of human rights, Voltaire doubted that ordinary people could be educated enough to make good political decisions. Unlike Montesquieu, he favored an enlightened absolutist monarchy over a mixed system of government.

Jean-Jacques Rousseau, perhaps the most widely known French writer of the period, was frequently at odds with Voltaire, but the two shared a reputation for having defended the cause of the oppressed. In his *Discourse on the Origins of Inequality,* Rousseau suggested that humanity had been better off when societies had been simpler and life more natural. His best-selling novels, *The New Héloise* and *Émile,* offered models of life lived according to the dictates of pure, natural feelings. More than Montesquieu and Voltaire, Rousseau urged readers to change the way they lived their private lives: his eloquent defense of "natural" motherhood and breast-feeding in *Émile* led many women readers to take a closer interest in raising their children, although his writings were also one of the sources of arguments that women's activities should be limited to the domestic sphere. But Rousseau was also concerned with more abstract political questions. His most important political work, *The Social Contract,* attempted to explain how men in complex, modern societies could retain a sense of enjoying their natural rights, provided they were able to participate effectively in governing themselves. Whereas Montesquieu had argued that liberty depended on limits and divisions of power, Rousseau claimed that it depended on the citizens' uniting to follow the dictates of their common interest, which he called the *general will.* He insisted on the importance of equality and shared values among the citizens of a good society, even suggesting that those who didn't accept the religion of the state might be put to death. Rousseau himself feared social upheaval, but his ideas took on a new resonance in 1789 when the French people found themselves facing the challenge of making a new political system. After his death in 1778, Rousseau's influence was extended by the publication of his *Confessions*, the first modern French autobiography. His detailed account of his personal life implied that even the stories of ordinary people's experiences deserved attention, and the slights he had suffered from aristocrats and officials made him a powerful icon for social justice.

The ideas of Montesquieu, Voltaire, and Rousseau were all reflected in a massive collaborative publication, the *Encyclopédie,* or *Encyclopedia,* edited by the philosophes Jean d' Alembert and Denis Diderot and published in installments between 1751 and 1765. The contributors to the *Encyclopédie* applied the critical and rational approach of the Enlightenment to the full range of human knowledge and to every aspect of society. In articles carefully crafted to pass the censors, they cast doubt on Church dogmas and raised questions about traditional political institutions. Detailed descriptions and illustrations of farming and manufacturing processes suggested both that manual labor—and the lower classes who performed it—deserved respect and that a scientific approach to production could improve efficiency. Another best seller of the period was the abbé Raynal's *History of the Two Indies,* a multivolume account of the creation of the European colonial empires. Raynal's book, which appeared in many editions in the 1770s and 1780s, questioned the right of European countries to govern overseas territories, and some of its passages denounced the injustice of slavery and predicted an eventual slave rebellion.

The Growth of Public Opinion

The readers of these Enlightenment works were part of the growing public whose collective opinion loomed ever larger in national life after the middle of the century. The phrase "public opinion" entered common use in France around 1750, reflecting this new reality. It referred to what was taken to be the general outlook of the men and women who discussed cultural and political issues in the increasing number of institutions that fostered such interchange. In Paris, writers, artists, and cultured nobles and bourgeois came together regularly in *salons,* informal weekly meetings often organized by active and intelligent women who used this means to obtain a degree of influence normally denied to them. Poems and essays first read in the salons often appeared later in one of the rapidly growing number of periodicals that were increasingly rivaling books as the elite's favorite form of reading material. Reading rooms, where for a small fee one could peruse a wide range of journals and books, also spread from Paris to most other French cities and towns. Provincial cities competed to build theaters, where performances of plays and concerts enlivened social life. The Masonic movement, introduced from England in the 1730s, was another important form of urban sociability. Masonic lodges propagated an ideology of equality. Members addressed each other as "brothers" regardless of their social rank, even though the membership in any given lodge tended to be socially homogeneous.

Participants in this increasingly lively network of cultural institutions read the works of the philosophes, such as Montesquieu, Voltaire, and Rousseau, but they also read a host of other texts. France's politically informed public developed first in reaction to controversies spawned by quarrels inspired by the Jansenist movement for spiritual reform within the Catholic Church. Jansenists sought a purer, more rigorous faith. They blamed the papacy for corrupting the Church. Louis XIV feared that the zealous advocates of this movement would undermine France's religious unity. In 1713, his lobbying led the papacy to issue an official condemnation of Jansenist doctrines, known as the bull *Unigenitus.* For the next sixty years, the French government and the Catholic hierarchy tried to root out Jansenist dissidence among French Catholics. Persecuted Jansenists found protectors among the judges of the parlements, who used the issue to cast themselves as defenders of the rights of individuals against arbitrary authority. Pro-Jansenist tracts were probably more effective than the abstract treatises of Montesquieu and Rousseau in convincing the French public of the need for fixed constitutional laws and of institutions to defend them.

Enthusiasm for the American Revolution also spread new ideas among the French public; sales of newspapers soared during the years when French troops and ships were supporting the colonists across the Atlantic. Benjamin Franklin, the American representative in Paris, skillfully promoted the idea that his countrymen and their institutions embodied simple, natural virtues that contrasted with corrupt European institutions. Although support for the American cause was widespread in France, some observers, such as the former minister Turgot, criticized the new country's constitution for maintaining too many traditions inherited from the past. Real reform, Turgot argued, needed to be carried out according to rational principles such as those developed by French Enlightenment thinkers.

While the American Revolution inspired thoughts about political change, exposés of the private lives of royal ministers, royal mistresses, and even members of the royal family discredited the government in France. Scurrilous *libelles* retailed unsavory details about the past of the aging Louis XV's last mistress, Madame du Barry, and titillated the public with hints about the difficulties that the young Louis XVI experienced in consummating his marriage with Marie-Antoinette, whose extravagant taste in clothes also came in for harsh criticism. In 1785, scandal touched the queen directly: she was accused of having encouraged the dissolute Cardinal Rohan to purchase a fabulously expensive diamond necklace as a gift for her. This "Diamond Necklace Affair" made the king look like a cuckold, unable to perform his basic functions as both husband and member of the royal dynasty, and helped undermine the sacred status of the monarchy. The scandal also reflected a widespread suspicion of women's influence in public affairs. Many critics claimed that a desire to please women had made all of French society "effeminate." By casting a bishop in the role of would-be seducer of the queen, the Diamond Necklace Affair also tarnished the Church. Writers like Voltaire and Rousseau had attacked religious orthodoxy on intellectual grounds, but the move away from strict Catholic belief had broader origins. Paradoxically, the Jansenist campaign for a more intense and spiritual faith may have contributed to the change in atmosphere. Jansenist zealotry, at its height in the first half of the eighteenth century, was too demanding for many Catholics and sometimes turned them against the Church altogether. Although attendance at services was still legally required until the Revolution, the decline in the number of wills leaving money for masses for the soul of the deceased after 1750 showed that a process of secularization was already under way in many regions of the country.

This process of secularization affected not only the elites who read Enlightenment literature but also sections of the lower classes. Demographic studies show growing intervals between births in peasant families in several regions, a sign of willingness to ignore the Church's prohibition against contraceptive practices. Nor was this the only area in which the lower orders showed an increasing tendency to think for themselves. The frequency with which peasant communities and urban artisan groups brought lawsuits against seigneurs and employers testifies to a conviction that even humble subjects had legal rights and a growing expectation that the government would enforce them, even against the powerful. (In the countryside, royal officials, aware that it was in their interest to protect tax-paying peasants against tax-protected seigneurs, sometimes encouraged peasant suits.) Changes in the realm of private life, such as the growing availability of inexpensive, colorful clothing, gave the urban poor more chance to think of themselves as individuals capable of making choices. More literate members of the population learned to express themselves by participating in the numerous essay competitions sponsored by provincial academies, which often challenged them to propose reforms to address social and economic problems. All of these developments reflected cultural changes that historians have increasingly come to see as giving the population a sense that its conditions of life could be considerably improved. When the steadily worsening financial crisis finally forced the French monarchy to allow the population to express its views in 1788, the king's ministers soon learned that no sector of the French population was prepared to accept changes from above without questioning them. Nobles, peasants, and all groups in between recognized that they had interests to defend and took active measures to protect them. The resulting debate revealed the extent to which traditional cultural values had already been undermined by the impact of the philosophes' writings and other cultural changes over the course of the century. The crisis of the French Revolution had deep roots in the country's past, but in 1787, no one could have predicted how drastically France's political, social, and cultural institutions would be reshaped once the Revolution began.

Critical Thinking Questions

1. The French monarchy faced many challenges in the second half of the eighteenth century. Explain how the structure of French society made it difficult for royal ministers to carry out reforms that might have warded off a revolution.
2. All major groups in the French population during the last decades of the Old Regime expressed dissatisfaction with the prevailing situation. Identify the main social groups making up prerevolutionary society, and the particular grievances that each of them had against existing institutions.
3. New ways of thinking led much of the French population to question existing institutions during the second half of the eighteenth century. Analyze the ways in which the ideas of the Enlightenment challenged political, religious, and social institutions, and how the notion of public opinion acquired a new importance in this period.

Notes

1. Cited in the University of Chicago College History Staff, eds., *History of Western Civilization* (Chicago: University of Chicago Press, 1977), 57.
2. Alexis de Tocqueville, *The Old Regime and the French Revolution* (New York: Doubleday, 1955), 177.
3. Jacques Ménétra, *Journal of My Life,* trans. Arthur Goldhammer (New York: Columbia University Press, 1986), 171.
4. Citations from Robert and Elborg Forster, eds., *European Society in the Eighteenth Century* (New York: Harper and Row, 1969), 40; and John Lough, *France on the Eve of Revolution* (Chicago: Dorsey, 1987), 34.

CHAPTER 2

The Collapse of the Absolute Monarchy, 1787–1789

LEARNING OBJECTIVES

After studying this chapter, you will be able to:

- **Explain why the king's ministers were compelled to start the "prerevolution" by calling an Assembly of Notables and then holding elections for the Estates-General.**
- **Describe how the elections to the Estates-General brought the French people into the realm of politics.**
- **Define the significance of the creation of the National Assembly and the popular violence of the storming of the Bastille and the "Great Fear" in the countryside.**

France in the mid-1780s was a society afflicted with numerous tensions. Nevertheless, it was not obvious that the country was on the brink of a revolutionary explosion. Despite the economic difficulties of the 1770s and 1780s, most peasants were better off than their ancestors under Louis XIV. Successful members of the bourgeoisie continued to enrich themselves and find ways to gain noble status. The questioning of traditional values had not given rise to any organized subversive movement. Repeated political crises had tested the institutions of absolutism, but each time the monarchy had emerged intact. Long-term trends had made a major crisis in France possible, but it took a specific set of events to make it unavoidable.

The Prerevolution

The most important of the events leading to a revolution was the fact that by late 1786, the French government was finally on the verge of complete insolvency. Charles Alexandre de Calonne, controller-general since 1783, had initially won his job because he promised that he could deal with the monarchy's financial problems without proposing controversial reforms. He had tried to keep his promises by engaging in a number of risky financial gambles, many of which increased France's foreign debts and reinforced criticism of the government's management of the economy. He finally found himself having to persuade Louis XVI of the necessity for extraordinary measures to head off bankruptcy. The immediate problem was the need to repay loans floated to fund France's participation in the American War of Independence: the fiscal crisis was thus directly linked to the effort to maintain France's role as a world power. But Calonne now advised Louis XVI that "the only way to bring real order into the finances is to revitalize the entire state by reforming all that is defective in its constitution."[1] Convinced that he could not accomplish his aims through the normal institutions of the monarchy, Calonne took the first step that was to lead to a revolution: he persuaded the king to convoke an Assembly of Notables to discuss fundamental changes in the structure of French government.

The convocation of the Assembly of Notables in January 1787 was the first of a series of events that historians have come to label the "prerevolution." During this period, which lasted from the beginning of 1787 until the meeting of the Estates-General in May 1789, the formal powers of the king and his ministers remained intact, and their bureaucratic machine continued to go through its regular routines. The authority of the absolutist state had not yet completely broken down, but it was rapidly eroding. In their efforts to escape from the looming shadow of bankruptcy, Calonne and his successors proposed more and more drastic reforms, throwing into question more and more of France's traditional institutions. By raising so many controversial issues, these initiatives galvanized ever-wider circles of the population into organized political action, until the king's call for nationwide elections to the Estates-General extended the process of politicization to every single town and village in France.

The great mid-twentieth-century French historian Georges Lefebvre labeled the prerevolution an "aristocratic revolution" because the most vocal opposition to royal reform initiatives during this period came from members of France's titled elite rather than from the representatives of the bourgeoisie and the lower classes, who were to take leading roles in events from 1789 onward. Lefebvre and other historians of the Marxist school interpreted the activity of aristocratic leaders during the prerevolution as the culmination of a longer process of "feudal reaction," an effort by the landowning class, threatened by the development of capitalism and an aggressive bourgeoisie, to shore up its slipping economic and social position.

More recent scholars have questioned the reality of this "feudal reaction." Nobles continued to look out for their economic interests, as they always had, but there is little evidence that this process had become more intense just before 1789 or that most nobles thought their position was in danger. The judges of the parlements and other aristocrats who challenged royal authority during the prerevolution were reacting primarily to a political threat. Like the royal ministers whom they opposed, they also recognized the need for major reforms. But they argued that the discredited absolutist system could not be trusted to remake itself. They opposed measures that they feared would increase ministerial power and insisted that the French "nation" be consulted about fundamental changes in its constitution. And they saw themselves as the natural spokesmen for the rest of the population.

The Assembly of Notables

By convening an assembly of carefully chosen noblemen, clergy, and high officials to examine his reform proposals, Calonne believed that he could enlist the force of public opinion in favor of his proposals. He wanted a new land tax that would be paid by all property owners—nobles, clergy, and commoners—and the establishment of representative assemblies in all of France's provinces. The land tax implied the abolition of the privileges that had set the nobles and clergy apart from the rest of the population; the provincial assemblies undermined the fundamental principle of absolutism that authority should flow from the top down. Calonne promised that his proposals would benefit all classes of the population and told the Notables, "Surely no selfish interest will oppose the general interest." But the 142 delegates who arrived in Versailles in February 1787 reacted to Calonne's projects with suspicion. Since taking office in 1783, Calonne had borrowed and spent freely, insisting that royal finances were healthy. Now he had suddenly reversed course, announcing that the treasury was empty and asking for new taxes. Few of the Notables were prepared to believe his claims without verification. Before they endorsed proposals that would overturn long-standing traditions and weaken their special privileges, they demanded a precise accounting of government revenue and expenditures.

Calonne responded by appealing to the public. He had his proposals printed, together with an introduction condemning the Notables for their defense of outmoded privileges. But the population was not ready to rally to the support of a notoriously high-handed minister against the Notables, who cast themselves as defenders of the people's traditional legal rights. By April 1787, it was clear that Calonne's gamble had failed. Louis XVI replaced him with one of his chief critics among the Notables, the archbishop of Toulouse, Loménie de Brienne. Brienne found the Assembly of Notables equally difficult to work with, however. Its members made it increasingly clear that they would not take the responsibility for approving new taxes. The most outspoken of them challenged the government to convene an elected assembly representing all elements of the population: the Estates-General of the realm, which had not met since 1614.

Brienne was reluctant to make such a complete departure from the policies of absolutism. Instead, he sought to get the parlements to approve modified versions of Calonne's proposals. Implementation of the plans for provincial assemblies and the creation of new municipal councils began, giving local elites a first taste of participatory politics. By a combination of concessions and pressure, Brienne worked out a delicate compromise with the parlements. In return for their approval of an extension of tax surcharges imposed during the American war, Brienne promised to convoke the Estates-General in 1792, by which time he calculated that the worst of the government's fiscal problems would be solved. When the Paris parlement met on 19 November 1787 to ratify this plan, however, Louis XVI upset all of his minister's hard work. Instead of allowing the judges of the parlement to discuss it freely, as they had been promised, the king ordered them to register it without a vote. "It is legal because I wish it," he insisted, reasserting the basic premise of absolutist government. His unexpected intervention outraged the judges and much of the public.

Compromise with the parlements having failed, Brienne and his fellow ministers decided on a policy of confrontation. On 8 May 1788, they promulgated a set of edicts that abolished the parlements, replacing them with a single high court for the whole country. They accompanied this radical measure with other reforms designed to make the elimination of the parlements more palatable to public opinion, such as the abolition of the fees that litigants had to pay to judges to have their cases heard. But these did little to soften the shock of their actions, which revived the fear of an all-powerful despotism raised by Chancellor Maupeou's efforts to remodel the parlements in 1770–1771. The country was flooded with pamphlets that restated the traditional "parlementary" or "magisterial" themes of the need to restore a balance in the constitution by limiting royal authority.

From Failed Reforms to Revolutionary Crisis

The attempt to abolish the parlements opened a debate that went beyond the issues of new taxes or court reform. At issue now was the question of who had the sovereign power to make fundamental laws for the kingdom. Supporters of the parlements maintained that this power could be exercised only by the nation itself, not by the king and his ministers. Inspired in part by the examples of England and the United States, these protesters demanded a form of representative government for France. French historical tradition offered a model of such a body: the Estates-General, a body of representatives chosen from the three traditional estates with the power to present grievances to the king and to consent to taxes.

As the resistance to the abolition of the parlements and the demands for a representative assembly mounted, the king and his ministers finally saw no alternative to convening the Estates-General. Royal authority was breaking down in several provinces, notably in Dauphiné, where, on 7 June 1788, "the day of the tiles," pro-parlement rioters hurling stones from rooftops drove royal troops out of the city of Grenoble in the first outbreak of the political violence that would mark the Revolution. On 5 July 1788, to answer these protests, Brienne announced that the Estates-General would be convened as soon as possible. He also suspended the censorship laws, allowing free public discussion of political matters. This announcement weakened government authority even further. By early August, the treasury was virtually empty, and Brienne had to resign in favor of the former minister Jacques Necker, who had a reputation as a reformer. His appointment, together with the recall of the parlements, produced a temporary calming effect, allowing the elections of deputies to the Estates-General to proceed.

Preparations for the Estates-General took place in the middle of a serious economic and social crisis. Many French manufacturers and workers were suffering from the effects of a free-trade treaty with England that Calonne had negotiated in 1786. In July 1788, a catastrophic hailstorm damaged grain crops across northern France, sending bread prices soaring as merchants anticipated a bad harvest. The archbishop of Paris, the Royal Society of Agriculture, and even the king, who announced the creation of a special lottery to raise money for the poor, tried to reassure the public, but there was no hiding the fact that the country faced its most threatening subsistence crisis in decades. These worsening economic conditions created an atmosphere of social unrest that added a sense of urgency to the meeting of the Estates-General.

The Meeting of the Estates-General

The summoning of the Estates-General raised a new and divisive question: How was the assembly to be organized? In previous centuries, the Estates-General had met in three separate chambers representing, respectively, the clergy, the nobility, and the Third Estate or commoners. All three chambers had to agree before the Estates-General could pass any resolution. Under these rules, the two privileged estates—the clergy and the nobles—who collectively amounted to less than 3 percent of the population, could dominate the proceedings. This perspective suited many of those who saw arbitrary authority as the country's main problem. They saw the nobles, particularly the aristocratic judges of the parlements, as the natural leaders of the nation and its protectors against the king's arbitrary power. On 25 September 1788, the newly restored Paris parlement explicitly ordered that the Estates-General meet "according to the forms of 1614"—that is, with the three orders meeting and voting separately. The judges were probably concerned primarily with preventing the government from setting its own rules for the meeting. But the effect of their edict was to change the main focus of political debate. Arguments between supporters and opponents of royal authority gave way to heated disputes between defenders of the aristocracy and the politically articulate members of the Third Estate, who now feared that their interests would be ignored at the upcoming assembly. The parlement's decree also caused protests in France's colonies, which had not existed in 1614: wealthy plantation owners insisted that they were too important to France's economy to be left unrepresented.

Movements in the provinces offered two different models of relationships between the privileged orders and the Third Estate. In Dauphiné, reformers under the leadership of a lawyer named Joseph Mounier drafted a plan to restore its long-dormant Estates in the form of a single assembly in which half the deputies would be chosen by the two privileged orders and half by the Third Estate. They defended their plan on the grounds that, like the English constitution, it would ensure harmony among the three Estates by giving the privileged orders a stake in the new system. Events in Brittany pointed in a very different direction. In this province, dominated by impoverished petty noblemen who feared seeing themselves displaced by wealthy urban commoners such as the wealthy merchants of the port city of Nantes, the privileged orders rejected any concessions to the Third Estate. Their opponents countered by urging the Third Estate to claim more authority for itself. In December and January, violence flared in the streets of Rennes, the provincial capital, as supporters and opponents of the nobility battled each other.

The Breton Third Estate's argument against the privileged orders was transferred to the national level in one of the most influential pamphlets written in the late fall of 1788, the abbé Sieyès's *What Is the Third Estate?* Sieyès began with a ringing declaration: "The plan of this work is very simple. We have three questions to ask: 1st. What is the Third Estate? Everything. 2nd. What has it been in the political order up to now? Nothing. 3rd. What does it demand? To become something." The Third Estate, Sieyès asserted, "has...within itself all that is necessary to constitute a complete nation," since its members did all the useful work in the country. "If the privileged order were abolished," he concluded, "the nation would be not something less but something more." He called for a single assembly representing those who made real contributions to the public welfare, from the humble peasant to the wealthy merchant and the learned lawyer. This group, Sieyès maintained, had a single common interest: "it is the nation."[2] Its representatives had every right to proceed on their own, disregarding any objections of deputies from the privileged orders. Other "patriotic" pamphleteers, such as the Protestant minister Rabaut Saint-Etienne, seconded Sieyès's arguments and added their own. Rabaut, for example, urged his readers not to "follow the conduct of your ancestors," but to be guided by "good sense" and "the law of nature." (See Document B.)

As the elections to the Estates-General proceeded in the first four months of 1789, compromise between the privileged orders and the Third Estate still seemed possible. A second Assembly of Notables, held in November and December 1788, rejected proposals that would have given the Third Estate more influence, but Necker managed to get Louis XVI to take a more conciliatory line by announcing the "doubling of the Third" on 27 December 1788: as in the Dauphiné assembly, the commoners would elect twice as many deputies as each of the other two orders. This decree dodged the question of whether the 600 deputies from the Third Estate and the 300 from each of the other two orders would meet together in a single assembly or in separate chambers, in which case the Third Estate's larger numbers would be meaningless.

DOCUMENT B

The Revolutionary Spirit in 1788

Together with the abbé Sieyès's *What Is the Third Estate?* the future deputy Rabaut Saint-Etienne's *Considerations on the Interests of the Third Estate* provided the clearest statement of the revolutionary challenge to France's existing institutions that developed in the months before the meeting of the Estates-General. In this excerpt, Rabaut Saint-Etienne expresses the revolutionaries' general attitude toward the past and calls on the Third Estate to adopt a new mentality. His appeal to the universal "law of nature" foreshadowed revolutionary claims that the principles adopted in France ought to be extended to the rest of humanity.

"It is obvious that there is only one real interest, and that is the interest of all. Where the interest of all is not properly understood. . . , one should at least follow the interest of the largest number. The largest number is the Third Estate composed of twenty-five million subjects, as against five or six hundred thousand with privileges. The distinction of ranks does not justify any distinction of political rights. If there were such a distinction, it would be unjust that power should belong to the smallest group, and this sub-aristocracy would be unconstitutional. Since national assemblies are assemblies of taxpayers, only taxpayers should be included, and those who do not pay taxes should not be included. Since those who are included have this right only as taxpayers, and therefore form only one category, the Estates-General are only a single body, a body of taxpayers."

"These are the true principles, this is your code, these are your true instructions, Third Estate, and I invite you to meditate on them. Don't bother to open your books, you will find them full of contradictions. Don't try to follow the conduct of your ancestors, they had no principles to follow and they were degraded. Don't ask what was done before, because you know what it was: you were sacrificed. Consult only good sense, which is the same in all countries and all epochs, and the law of nature, the basis of all rights, whose principles can never be overridden."

(From Rabaut Saint-Etienne, *Considerations sur les intérêts du Tiers-Etat* [1788] pp. 35–37. Translation by Jeremy D. Popkin.)

The elections to the Estates-General transformed the notion of government according to public opinion from an abstract slogan into a living reality. In every parish and district of the country, all adult men—and, in exceptional cases, a few women—were called together not only to choose representatives but also to voice their views on what issues the Estates-General should consider by drawing up *cahiers de doléance,* or lists of grievances. The cahiers provided a complex and ambiguous picture of the population's concerns on the eve of the Revolution. All three orders' cahiers indicated a consensus in favor of major constitutional reforms, above all the creation of a system of representative government that would limit the king's powers. The nobility and clergy were ready to accept some major modifications of their privileges, such as equality of taxation. There was strong sentiment for reform of the legal system, and most nobles joined the Third Estate in favoring abolition of censorship. The nobility's cahiers hardly foresaw the complete abolition of their order, however, and the clergy opposed the creation of an essentially secular society.

Cahiers representing peasant villages mixed appeals for broad reform with local concerns, calling for repair of bridges, abolition of specific tolls and dues, and measures against specific privilege-holders, such as the postmaster of the village of Ecommoy whose neighbors complained that he was evading taxes. Taken as a whole, they represented a serious protest against the workings of the seigneurial system and the privileges of the nobility. As deputies from the villages came together to elect regional representatives, members of the urban Third Estate, usually bourgeois lawyers, office-holders, and other professionals, reworked these demands, giving them a more general form. Even so, the Third Estate cahiers were still something less than a revolutionary program. They revealed strong dissatisfaction with existing conditions and a widespread demand for the end of many special privileges, but they did not call for the elimination of social distinctions or the abolition of the monarchy. The summoning of the Estates-General raised special controversies in France's colonies, where white colonists feared that the campaign for liberty in France itself would lead to an attack on slavery. Some colonists demanded the right to elect deputies to the Estates-General to protect their interests. While the cahiers were generally moderate in tone and content, the lifting of censorship and the general atmosphere of excitement encouraged the circulation of pamphlets that demanded more radical reforms, sometimes in violent language. This pamphlet literature showed that cautious compromises would not satisfy the public's hunger for real change.

The Parliamentary Revolution

On 3 May 1789, the approximately 1,200 deputies to the Estates-General assembled in Versailles. Some were already well known because of their role in the public debates that had occupied the country ever since Calonne had convoked his Assembly of Notables more than two years earlier, whereas others were obscure parish priests, provincial noblemen, and small-town lawyers. Contrary to the allegations of critics then and since, many of the members of the Estates-General had practical experience in public affairs as royal officials, in local government, or as administrators in the Church. Among the assembled deputies, there was an articulate minority of self-proclaimed Patriots, bent on a sweeping transformation of French public life. Their program included a fixed, written constitution for France that would severely limit the king's powers, the abolition of legal privileges, a representative assembly, and a "declaration of rights" that would guarantee religious toleration and press freedom. Many of the Patriot leaders were also members of the Society of Friends of the Blacks, an organization founded in 1788 to oppose slavery. The Society was one of the first groups to introduce the language of natural rights into political debates.

Initially, however, most of the deputies rejected the Patriots' radicalism and looked for leadership to Louis XVI, whose popularity had soared since he had agreed to the convocation of the Estates-General, and to the chief minister, Necker. Necker's budgetary wizardry, the deputies assumed, would produce a solution to the fiscal crisis. Unfortunately for the monarchy, the king and Necker proved unprepared for the extraordinary situation they now found themselves in. Louis, an honest and well-meaning man, lacked the vision and determination to take the lead in a radical reform movement; Necker had little sense of how to handle a crisis. Charged with presenting the government's program to the Estates-General in its opening session, he exhausted the deputies' patience with a long-winded account of the monarchy's fiscal problems but offered them no specific proposals to debate. The king and Necker left the Estates-General itself to decide the burning question of whether to vote by head or by order. With no commitment to significant reform from the king, the deputies of the Third Estate had every reason to fear that subsequent proceedings would be dominated by the two privileged orders. This fear drove even the moderate members of the Third Estate to support a radical decision: the Third Estate immediately paralyzed the assembly by refusing to organize itself and begin work unless the other two orders agreed to meet and vote in common. The underlying issue was fundamental: was France to become a country of citizens enjoying equal rights, or was it to remain divided into groups with differing privileges?

On 10 June, after five weeks of futile negotiations with the other orders, the Third Estate deputies had become sufficiently impatient to endorse a radical suggestion from the abbé Sieyès. The Third Estate sent a final invitation to the nobles and the clergy to form a single assembly, announcing that it would proceed without them if they declined. Joined by a handful of deputies from the clergy, the Third Estate deputies voted on 17 June 1789 rename themselves the "National Assembly," thus proclaiming that they were speaking for the national community as a whole. News of their actions reached a wider public through the regular letters that many of the deputies sent home and via hastily created newspapers that summarized the Estates-General's debates. In coffeehouses and public places throughout the nation, ordinary citizens, living embodiments of the public opinion that had taken on a new level of importance with the monarchy's virtual abdication of power, voiced their support for the deputies.

The Third Estate's decision to transform itself into a National Assembly was a challenge to the authority of Louis XVI as well as to the other two orders. Three days later, on 20 June, the king tried to regain control of the situation by calling a special session of all three orders on 23 June. In the meantime, royal officials locked the deputies of the National Assembly out of their regular meeting hall. Fearing that the king would try to quash their decisions, the members of the Assembly held an emergency session in the only building they could find that was large enough to accommodate them, the king's indoor tennis court. There, they swore the dramatic "Oath of the Tennis Court," pledging not to cease meeting until they had given France a new constitution.

At the royal session on 23 June 1789, the king proposed limited reforms but insisted that the deputies continue meeting in separate assemblies. When royal officials ordered the deputies to disperse after the king's speech, Count Mirabeau, a "Patriot" nobleman who had been elected to represent the Third Estate of his native Provence and who had already established himself as one of the National Assembly's leaders, defiantly replied, "We are here by the will of the French people, and we will only be dispersed by the force of bayonets." Faced with the intransigence of the Third Estate deputies, the king was forced to back down. On 27 June 1789, he himself ordered the deputies of the clergy and the nobility to join the National Assembly. The former deputies of the Third Estate seemed to have won, and the National Assembly started work on a constitution. But the bayonets to which Mirabeau had referred were not out of the picture. The government had begun to assemble troops near the capital; the incipient revolution still risked being put down by force.

The Storming of the Bastille

While the troops assembled and the deputies debated, the rest of the French population intervened to determine the country's fate. The agitation accompanying the elections to the Estates-General and the unrest stemming from difficult economic conditions had already led to popular insurrections in several parts of the country. In March and April, a wave of riots swept the region around Marseille, and in April 1789, artisans and workers in Paris's populous Faubourg Saint-Antoine sacked the mansion of the wallpaper manufacturer Reveillon, who had been accused of trying to lower wages. These violent incidents showed the strength of social tensions. Political excitement also ran high. Crowds gathered every day in open spaces like the gardens of the Palais-Royal to listen to reports from Versailles and speeches by self-appointed orators. Popular sympathies were overwhelmingly with the leaders of the Third Estate and hostile to the "aristocrats" opposing them. Political agitation affected even the soldiers stationed in and around Paris, some of whom openly expressed their sympathies for the National Assembly.

In Versailles, however, the king's most conservative advisers had gained the upper hand. On 11 July 1789, Louis dismissed Necker, who, in spite of his ineffectual performance at the opening of the Estates-General, had still been regarded as an advocate of reform. Even before the deputies in Versailles could respond to this move, the people of Paris took to the streets in protest. On 12 and 13 July, as fears grew that the troops ringing the capital would be sent in to put down the patriotic movement, crowds besieged the royal arsenals in the city, demanding arms. They also destroyed the tax-collection barriers that formed a wall around the city, expressing their determination to demand changes that would make concrete changes in their lives. Meanwhile, army commanders warned Versailles that they could not count on their men to fight against the Parisians.

On 14 July 1789, a large crowd composed primarily of skilled artisans and shopkeepers, aided by soldiers from one of the regiments stationed in the city, surrounded the Bastille, an imposing medieval fortress-prison that had become a symbol of despotic authority. Defended by only a few hundred troops and housing only seven prisoners at that moment, the Bastille had little military significance, but when the

THE AWAKENING OF THE THIRD ESTATE

This caricature was one of many that communicated the significance of the dramatic events of July 1789 even to those who could not read. In this striking image, representatives of the nobility and the clergy recoil in alarm as a figure representing the commoners of the Third Estate frees himself from his chains and prepares to take up arms. In the background, supporters of the Revolution are demolishing the fortress of the Bastille and carrying the severed heads of royal officials killed in the uprising.

Parisians, infuriated by the commander's refusal to give up the weapons it contained, stormed and captured it, their victory became an immediate symbol of the newly born popular revolutionary movement. News of the day's events shocked the king and his advisors, who abandoned any hope of crushing that movement by force. The National Assembly now had the support it needed to move forward, but the deputies recognized that they would have to reckon with their popular allies' demands. (See Document C.)

The storming of the Bastille was accompanied by the killing of several officials of the Old Regime, showing how quickly popular action could turn to violence. The victims' severed heads were carried through the streets in a gory celebration of the popular victory. The reform-minded Patriot leaders who had helped set off the insurrection moved quickly to restore order, however. The committee of electors who had chosen Paris's deputies to the Estates-General turned themselves into an improvised city government, choosing one of their members, the astronomer Jean-Sylvain Bailly, as mayor. They created a civic militia, the National Guard, to maintain order in the streets; it was put under the command of Lafayette, the reform-minded nobleman famous for his participation in the American Revolution. From the outset, it was clear that there was a potential cleavage between leaders like Bailly and Lafayette, willing to

DOCUMENT C

The Revolutionary Explosion in Paris , 12–14 July 1789

On 12 July 1789, Parisians learned that the king had dismissed the popular minister Necker from office. An eyewitness describes how the future revolutionary journalist Camille Desmoulins roused the crowd in the Palais Royal gardens.

"A young man, standing on a table, cried 'To arms!' drew his sword, showed a pistol and a green cockade. The crowd listening to him . . . imitated him by going from a deep silence to horrible cries. One came alive, one became excited, and the leaves of the trees, torn off in an instant, served as cockades for several thousand men. It was a true explosion, whose echo would last for three days." (J. B. Dusaulx, *L'Oeuvre de sept jours* [Paris, 1790]. Translation by Jeremy D. Popkin.)

The *Révolutions de Paris* was one of the first newspapers founded after 14 July 1789. Its breathless account of the capture of the Bastille reflects the electric atmosphere of the Revolution's first days.

"The action became ever more intense. The citizens no longer feared the gunfire. They scrambled all over the rooftops, into the rooms, and as soon as one of the garrison appeared on the tower, he attracted the fire of a hundred sharpshooters, who immediately knocked him down . . . Numerous women helped us with all their strength. Even children, after each salvo from the fort, ran here and there to pick up the cannonballs . . . We pressed ahead, we reached the staircase, we seized the prisoners, we penetrated everywhere. Some seized the guards, others scrambled to the top of the towers. They waved the country's sacred flag, to the cheers and the delight of an immense crowd. . . .

"This glorious day should astonish our enemies, and promise us the triumph of justice and liberty." (From *Révolutions de Paris,* no. 1 [12–19 July 1789]. Translation by Jeremy D. Popkin.)

Published in the Dutch city of Leiden, the *Gazette de Leyde* was Europe's most influential newspaper in 1789. Its comments on the storming of the Bastille show that the event stirred fears as well as hopes:

"It is time for the friends of true liberty to realize this truth, that unbridled license often overturns it at the moment when it could be established, the arbitrary power of the multitude being far more dangerous to it than that of despotism itself."

(From *Gazette de Leyde,* 31 July 1789. Translation by Jeremy D. Popkin.)

profit from the success of the popular movement but determined to keep it under control, and the mass of the population, whose direct action had ensured the revolutionary movement's success but who were now expected to return quietly to their homes.

A similar combination of elite and popular action characterized the wave of revolutionary uprisings that swept over other French cities in July 1789, some before and some after the Parisian events. Crowds assaulted local buildings that symbolized royal authority and forced the royal intendants and the appointed municipal officials to yield power to improvised councils of men loyal to the National Assembly. This "municipal revolution" paralyzed the royal administration and transferred responsibility for enforcing the laws to officials who owed their authority to the support of the local population, thereby reversing several centuries of administrative centralization.

Even more threatening to the traditional social order was the wave of peasant violence that followed the storming of the Bastille. In many rural regions, peasants, terrified by rumors that "brigands" in the pay of aristocratic opponents of the Revolution were about to devastate their crops, turned on the manor houses of the local nobles in a mass movement that came to be known as the "Great Fear."

Relatively few nobles were actually killed, but a number of chateaux were burned. More often, the rioting peasants forced local seigneurs to turn over the charters and deeds that consecrated their special privileges. "After having broken the locks on my cabinets that held my documents…, they burned them in the woods near my chateau," one noble victim complained.[3] The peasants' actions made it clear that they demanded an end to the exactions of the seigneurial system. This rural insurrection, the largest outbreak of peasant revolt in France in many centuries, completed the breakdown of royal authority. As a result, the National Assembly had the chance to make important reforms. But the deputies of the National Assembly, many of whom were themselves owners of rural property, faced the daunting challenge of restoring order not just in Paris and other towns but throughout the country.

As the authority of the government and the nobles dissolved, power shifted to those who declared their loyalty to the Assembly and adopted the new symbols of the Revolution, such as the red, white, and blue tricolor cockade that the Paris Patriots had created as a badge. This largely spontaneous movement from below ensured the success of the National Assembly and of what was now openly called a revolution. In the face of the crowd's actions in Paris, Louis XVI on 15 July 1789 announced the recall of his troops and the reappointment of Necker. Two days later, the king traveled to his capital city. Large crowds lined his route and applauded when he accepted a tricolor cockade from Bailly, the new mayor. Louis's action symbolized the reconciliation of the king and his people, once again joined together like a father and his children. But the atmosphere of euphoria and the applause for the monarch could not conceal the fact that the former absolute ruler had had to recognize the authority of an official installed by a popular insurrection.

Critical Thinking Questions

1. At the start of 1787, Louis XVI's ministers found themselves compelled to summon an Assembly of Notables and to appeal to the public to help solve the monarchy's problems. Why was the government forced to take such a step, and why did this decision further weaken the monarchy?
2. The elections to the Estates-General, held in the first months of 1789, brought the entire French population into politics for the first time. What were the major demands expressed during the election campaign? What changes in the system of absolute monarchy would they have required?
3. The Third Estate's decision to convert itself into a National Assembly and the storming of the Bastille on 14 July 1789, marked the beginning of the French Revolution. Why were these two events so important, and why did it take a combination of action by the deputies and by the common people to create the Revolution?

Notes

1. Cited in Jean Egret, *The French Pre-Revolution, 1787–1788,* Wesley D. Camp, trans. (Chicago: University of Chicago Press, 1977), 2.
2. Sieyès, cited in John Hall Stewart, *A Documentary Survey of the French Revolution* (New York: Macmillan, 1951), 42–44.
3. Cited in J. M. Roberts, ed., *French Revolution Documents* (Oxford: Basil Blackwell, 1966), 141.

CHAPTER 3

The Revolutionary Rupture, 1789–1790

LEARNING OBJECTIVES

After studying this chapter, you will be able to:

- **Describe the main provisions of the decrees abolishing privileges and the Declaration of the Rights of Man, and identify the principles underlying them.**
- **Explain the controversies over basic features of the new constitution, and the significance of the October Days uprising.**
- **Analyze the logic behind the revolutionary reform of the Church, and the arguments of those who opposed it.**

The Experience of Revolution

The dramatic events of July 1789 generated many slogans. One of the most expressive was the motto of the *Révolutions de Paris,* a weekly newspaper founded just after the storming of the Bastille: "*Les grands ne nous paraîssent pas grands que parce que nous sommes à genoux. Levons-nous!*" ("Those above us look powerful only because we are on our knees. Let's stand up!") In two short sentences, the anonymous creator of this slogan captured the essence of the experience that the French people had suddenly found themselves caught up in. By taking action—by getting off their knees and adopting a new posture—the participants in the Revolution changed their sense of who they were: instead of royal subjects, they became free citizens. They also imposed a new identity on their former overlords: *les grands* would no longer be *les grands* if they no longer towered over their supposed inferiors, and the hierarchies of power and privilege that had structured French society would cease to exist. The *Révolutions de Paris*'s motto provided a powerful definition of what carrying out a revolution meant.

Historians ever since have used the term *revolution* to describe the drama that began in 1789. In the era of the Renaissance, when history was seen as running in cyclical patterns, the concept of revolution implied a return to a prior state of things. By the eighteenth century, it had come to mean any sudden and unexpected political event. In this sense, revolutions were frequent and occurred, like natural disasters, without human intervention. In 1789, however, as historian Keith Baker has shown, the word quickly took on a new meaning. Rather than speaking of "revolutions" in the plural, the French and the foreign observers who followed the events in France with keen interest now spoke of "the Revolution," a unique and singular event. The French Revolution, furthermore, was an open-ended event that human beings shaped, not one they simply endured. The rapid adoption of this new terminology showed that contemporaries immediately recognized how profoundly the events of June and July 1789 had altered the way the French population understood its world.

As they recognized the extraordinary nature of their situation, the deputies of the National Assembly, along with much of the French population, were both excited and alarmed. Making a revolution offered the opportunity to create a new society, but it also risked plunging France into a violent breakdown. Conscious of what was at stake, the deputies moved rapidly to lay out the basic principles of a new society, strikingly different from the hierarchical world of the past. Within a few months they had abolished the absolute monarchy, the seigneurial system, and the complex of privileges that had pervaded French society. In their place, they had proclaimed the primacy of the rights of individual citizens and created a system of representative government to protect them. Completing the details of the new constitution would occupy the Assembly until September 1791, but the radical direction of its work was clear by the end of the summer of 1789.

The "Abolition of Feudalism" and the Declaration of Rights

In the weeks after the Paris crowd's storming of the Bastille on 14 July 1789, the 1,200 deputies to the National Assembly in Versailles had a remarkable opportunity. The king could no longer obstruct their work. His army and his bureaucracy had ceased to function, and the most ardent opponents of the Revolution, such as the king's younger brother, the Count of Artois, had fled abroad. The deputies could count on a national groundswell of popular support. But the violence that had resulted in the lynchings after the storming of the Bastille and the wave of peasant revolts in the countryside showed that events could easily escape the Assembly's control. The deputies needed to establish a new social and political order before the disintegration of the old one plunged France into chaos.

In August 1789, the deputies took two decisive steps that defined the ways in which the new society and the new government would differ from the old. The first was to eliminate the dense thicket of special privileges that had blocked all previous efforts at change. On the night of 4 August 1789, the Assembly, spurred by the reports of rural insurrection arriving from around the country, held a special session at which one of the liberal nobles planned to propose abolishing some of his order's privileges. The deputies hoped that this would satisfy the peasantry and end the burning of chateaux and legal documents. This limited reform was unexpectedly upstaged when another noble deputy made a sweeping proposal to do away with the whole complex of "feudal" rights. The success of this motion launched a chain reaction of further renunciations. Representatives of the clergy moved to abolish tithes; deputies from the provinces and privileged cities gave up their immunities from taxes and customs fees. The sale of government offices was done away with, and recruitment to Church, government, and military positions formerly reserved for nobles was thrown open to all citizens. By the time the exhausted deputies staggered out into the dawn on 5 August, they had gone far to "abolish the feudal regime entirely," as the preamble to their edicts promised.

The deputies later qualified much of the language they had initially voted for. Peasants, for instance, soon discovered that the National Assembly had made distinctions between "feudal" obligations supposedly derived from medieval serfdom and "real" obligations considered analogous to rent. Peasants were required to pay their landlords compensation for the abolition of "real" obligations. Nevertheless, the basic thrust of this radical package of reforms remained intact. The Assembly had decided that France would henceforth be a community of legally equal citizens. The centuries-old distinctions between clergy and laity, between social classes, and between the inhabitants of different regions of the kingdom had been leveled. No subsequent French regime has been able to reverse this fundamental accomplishment.

Having dismantled the old order, the National Assembly began establishing the new on 27 August 1789 when it endorsed the seventeen articles of the "Declaration of the Rights of Man and Citizen." (See Document D.) This document, the most important expression of the French Revolution, clearly defined the fundamental principles of a new society based on equality and individual rights and a new system of government based on the consent of the governed. Often described as the culmination of the intellectual movement of the Enlightenment, the Declaration reflected ideas about politics and society that had been discussed throughout the previous century. The deputies' effort to cast the Enlightenment's theoretical assumptions in the form of a short but comprehensive list of propositions forced them to confront difficulties that earlier writers had not always recognized.

The decision to enact a Declaration of Rights before any other part of the new constitution had been agreed on caused controversy. Many deputies feared that such a sweeping statement of principles would give ordinary citizens exaggerated notions of their rights. The Assembly's majority, however, decided that it would be riskier to start creating new institutions without having defined the basic principles they were supposed to reflect. Some of the Declaration's provisions were modeled after clauses in the bills of rights in the American state constitutions, but the procedure the Assembly adopted was the reverse of what the drafters of the American constitution, who worked in a calmer situation, were doing at almost the same time: only after finishing the federal constitution in 1787 did they propose a Bill of Rights, which was enacted in 1791 to limit the powers of the federal government.

The Declaration's eloquent preamble asserted that "ignorance, neglect, and scorn of the rights of man are the sole causes of public misfortunes," implying that the document itself would inaugurate a new historical era. Its first article echoed the opening sentence of Jean-Jacques Rousseau's *Social Contract* in proclaiming that "men are born and remain free and equal in rights." Article 2 listed the "natural" rights that governments were created to protect: "liberty, property, security, and resistance to oppression." Article 4 defined liberty in broad terms as "anything that does not harm another person." The full implications of this principle were not spelled out at the time, but it clearly suggested that each individual should have the right to make important decisions without interference from the government, from privileged corporate groups such as guilds, which would be formally abolished in 1791, or

THE DECLARATION OF RIGHTS

The Declaration of the Rights of Man and Citizen was as important for its symbolic power as for its specific contents. In this allegorical engraving, the Declaration of the Rights of Man and Citizen is shown separating the sunlit world of liberty from the dark realm of feudal rights and privileges, represented by the crawling figure in the lower left corner of the picture.

DOCUMENT D

The Declaration of the Rights of Man and Citizen, 1789

Although the deputies of the National Assembly considered the document they approved on 26 August 1789 as simply a working draft, which they expected to revise later, it immediately became the most authoritative statement of the French Revolution's principles. The Declaration forms part of the constitution of today's French Fifth Republic.

"The Representatives of the French People, having constituted themselves as a National Assembly, concluding that ignorance, forgetting, or disregard for the rights of man are the only causes of public misfortunes and the corruption of governments, have resolved to set out, in a solemn declaration, the natural, inalienable, and sacred rights of man, in order that this declaration, constantly in the minds of all members of society, will continually remind them of their rights and their duties; so that the actions of the legislative power and those of the executive power, evaluated at every moment in relationship to the purpose of all political institutions, will be more respected; so that the citizens' demands, based henceforth on simple and incontestable principles, will always tend to uphold the Constitution, for the benefit of all. In consequence, the National Assembly recognizes and declares, in the presence and under the auspices of the Supreme Being, the following rights of man and citizen."

Article 1: Men are born and remain free and equal in rights. Social distinctions can only be justified if they are useful to the community.

Article 2: The purpose of any political association is to protect the natural and imprescriptible rights of man. These rights are liberty, property, security, and resistance to oppression.

Article 3: The basis of all sovereignty resides essentially in the nation. No group, no individual can exercise any authority that does not expressly derive from it.

Article 4: Liberty consists in the power to do anything that does not harm others: thus, the rights of each man are restricted only by limits that assure other members of society the enjoyment of these same rights. These limits can only be set by the law.

Article 5: The law has the right to forbid only those actions harmful to society. Whatever is not forbidden by the law cannot be prohibited, and no one can be compelled to do anything it does not require.

Article 6: The law is the expression of the general will. All citizens have the right to participate personally, or through their representatives, in its establishment. It must be the same for all, whether it protects or punishes. All citizens being equal in its eyes, are equally eligible for all honors, appointments, and public positions, according to their capacities, and without regard to any distinction other than that of their virtues and their talents.

Article 7: No man can be indicted, arrested, or held except in the cases determined by the law, and according to the forms it has laid down. Those who solicit, transmit, carry out or have others carry out arbitrary orders should be punished; but any citizen summoned or seized according to the law must obey immediately: he makes himself guilty if he resists.

Article 8: The law can only establish punishments that are clearly and obviously necessary, and no one can be punished except by virtue of a law established and put into effect previous to the crime, and applied in a legal manner.

Article 9: Since every man is presumed innocent until he has been declared guilty, if it considered necessary to arrest him, any severity that is not necessary to secure his person must be rigorously repressed by the law.

Article 10: No one should be disturbed because of his opinions, even about religion, provided that their practice does not disturb the public order established by the law.

Article 11: Free communication of thoughts and opinions is one of the most precious rights of man: every citizen can therefore speak, write, publish freely, subject to responsibility for abuse of this freedom in cases determined by law.

Article 12: The protection of the rights of man and citizen requires a public force: this force is therefore established for the benefit of all, and not for the private advantage of those who exercise it.

Article 13: To pay for the public force, and for expenses of administration, a general tax is indispensable. It should be shared equally among the citizens, according to their means.

Article 14: All citizens have the right to ascertain, by themselves or through their representatives, of the necessity of the general tax, to freely consent to it, to know how it is used, and to decide on its rate, on what it should it be based, on the method of collection, and on its duration.

Article 15: Society has the right to require every public official to account for his administration.

Article 16: Any society in which the protection of rights is not assured, or the separation of power is not determined, has no constitution.

Article 17: Property being an inviolable and sacred right, no one can be deprived of it, except in cases where public necessity, legally established, clearly requires such action, and only on condition of a just and prior indemnity.

(Translation: Jeremy D. Popkin)

from parents, who had previously had significant power even over grown-up children. Other articles of the Declaration fleshed out the notions of liberty and security by giving citizens explicit protection against arbitrary arrest and promising them freedom of religious belief and freedom of expression. The Declaration's final article called property ownership an "inviolable and sacred right," but also allowed for its expropriation with proper compensation. This justified the abolition of seigneurial rights carried out on the night of August 4, but it opened the way to further debates about how the right of property might be limited in the public interest. Citizens' rights were to be protected not only by prohibitions against government intrusion but also by provisions giving them the right to participate in making laws and oversee their administration. Article 3 asserted that "the source of all sovereignty is located in essence in the nation," thereby transferring supreme authority from the king to the community of citizens. Article 6, again borrowing language from Rousseau, proclaimed that "law is the expression of the general will" and promised all citizens a right to participate in the political process. The statement that they had "the right to concur personally or through their representatives in its formation" straddled a crucial question, however. Rousseau had insisted that the only free people were those who participated personally in lawmaking, like the citizens of the ancient Greek city-states, all of whom voted in public meetings. The Declaration anticipated that citizens would delegate this power to elected representatives, but its wording allowed radical critics to insist that it could really be fulfilled only by a system of direct democracy. In addition to sharing in the making of the laws, the Declaration promised citizens that their representatives would have the right to approve taxes and expenditures and to review the conduct of public officials (Articles 14 and 15).

The Declaration's drafters saw a direct connection between liberty and equality: if all human beings possessed rights simply by virtue of being born, these rights necessarily had to be "the same for all," as Article 6 stated. This implied the ending of all special privileges, except those granted to public officials so that they could carry out their duties. Every citizen had the right to compete for "all honors, positions, and public employments," which were to be awarded solely on the basis of "virtues and talents," without regard to considerations such as noble birth.

Although most of their wording emphasized citizens' rights, the drafters of the Declaration believed in the necessity of government. They stressed that citizens were obliged to obey laws, pay taxes, and submit to arrest warrants "instantly." Article 12 called for the maintenance of a "public force" to uphold the law "for the advantage of all." The articles guaranteeing freedom of religion and the press contained clauses stating that even those fundamental rights could be limited by law. Article 16 tried to ensure that no future government would abuse these powers by setting conditions for recognizing a legitimate political system: it had to protect individual rights, and the powers of government had to be divided, in order to prevent any sort of tyranny. The later course of the Revolution would show that the drafters of the Declaration had been optimistic in assuming that this statement and the provisions on popular participation would prevent any oppression of the citizens.

It is hard to exaggerate the importance of the Declaration of Rights of Man and Citizen. Its seventeen articles explicitly condemned the basic ideas underlying absolute monarchy and social systems based on hierarchy and privilege. In their place, the Declaration called for a community of equal citizens endowed with extensive rights and a participatory political system meant to protect them. Unlike the American Bill of Rights, much of which refers to specific parts of the Federal constitution adopted in 1787, the French Declaration was formulated in abstract and universal terms, suggesting that its principles were valid not only for France but also for all other nations. Most historians have seen the Declaration as a fundamental source of modern ideas of human rights. In recent years, however, critics, such as Samuel Moyn, author of *The Last Utopia: Human Rights in History,* have argued that, by linking the possession of rights to citizenship status, the French revolutionaries made it too easy for governments to deny them to those who were excluded from the national community. Even at the time, it was recognized that the Declaration of the Rights of Man and Citizen incorporated significant ambiguities and failed to deal with some vital issues. Did the term "man" include all human beings or only members of the male sex? Were all men now full citizens? How was the promise of equality to be reconciled with the explicit defense of private property, the unequal distribution of which left some citizens better off than others? Did property include the black slaves in France's colonies? Did the repeated clauses stating that certain rights could be limited by law give the government too much power? Did the promise of liberty include the right to oppose the Revolution itself? And who was entitled to speak for the nation, the new repository of political legitimacy? Articles proposed at the time but not included in the Declaration suggested that society had a duty to provide help its members exercise their rights by ensuring them an education and a basic level of subsistence if they could not support themselves. Much more than the American Revolution, the French movement raised fundamental political questions.

The Constitutional Debates

By the fall of 1789, the 1,200 men who had arrived in Versailles at the beginning of May, uncertain about their role and for the most part unacquainted with one another, had found leaders and organized into informal parties. Those who considered themselves the most determined supporters of the Revolution stationed themselves in seats on the left side of the speaker's desk; the most vehement opponents of the Revolution claimed the right side of the room; and the terms "left" and "right" have served ever since to characterize radicals and conservatives, not only in France but also throughout the world. Although the Assembly had abolished the privileges of the nobles and the Church, the fact that half its members had originally been elected to represent those groups meant that it contained vocal spokesmen for conservative and moderate views.

The size and diversity of the Assembly made it difficult for any one deputy to dominate it. The strongest potential leader was Mirabeau. He was a master orator and also one of the first to sense the importance of the newspaper press. As early as May 1789, he had founded one of the first revolutionary journals. Mirabeau believed that the Revolution offered an opportunity, not to destroy the monarchy, but to strengthen it. By working with the Assembly to abolish outmoded institutions and to draft a constitution that would give him genuine powers, the king could win the country's trust. Mirabeau embarked on a delicate strategy of trying to control the National Assembly while simultaneously making secret efforts to persuade the king and queen to commit themselves to accept the basic results of the Revolution. "There is no hope for the State and for the king except in the closest possible alliance between the ruler and the people," he wrote to the king.[1] But Mirabeau's transparent personal ambition and his dissolute private life made other deputies distrustful of him. The Assembly's decision in November 1789 to prohibit any of its members from serving as royal ministers, as members of Parliament did in England, was aimed at keeping Mirabeau out of power.

No other deputy came close to obtaining sway over the Assembly and the revolutionary movement. Sieyès, whose ideas had had such influence during the critical days of June 1789, lacked speechmaking skills, and he soon dissipated much of his prestige by defending the Church's privileges. Lafayette, well-known because of his participation in the American War of Independence, lost much of his popularity because his position as commander of the Paris National Guard required him to repress public demonstrations in the capital. Some deputies, such as Maximilien Robespierre, a small-town lawyer from northern France who became the leading advocate of the common people's interests in the debates, and the abbé Maury, a clergyman from humble origins who became the most eloquent defender of royal authority and Church interests, established themselves as spokesmen for minority viewpoints. But the National Assembly, setting a precedent that has had lasting influence in France, made its decisions collectively, through debate and bargaining, and blocked the emergence of strong leaders.

The Assembly faced little competition from the king or his ministers. Louis XVI stubbornly resisted Assembly measures he regarded as undermining royal authority or religion, but he put forward no positive program. The queen, Marie-Antoinette, had a firmer character but a limited comprehension of the revolutionary situation. Her widely rumored efforts to get foreign powers to intervene against the Revolution made her and the monarchy increasingly unpopular. The king's ministers, so influential under the Old Regime, discovered that both the National Assembly and the population no longer respected their authority.

After the passage of the Declaration of the Rights of Man, the Assembly turned to the question of what powers the king should have in the new constitution. At first, a moderate group, the *monarchiens,* dominated the Assembly's constitutional committee. Their leaders included several reform-minded nobles and Joseph Mounier, the lawyer who had led the revolutionary movement in Dauphiné in 1788. The monarchiens epitomized the fusion of property-owning elites that had seemed poised to govern the country at the end of the Old Regime. The monarchiens' proposal promised the king significant powers: he would have a large budget to spend as he pleased and the right to veto laws he disapproved of. The legislature would have consisted of two houses, as in England, one of peers and another representing the common people. More radical deputies, including Mirabeau, rejected this scheme: they feared that the king would use his veto to paralyze the Assembly and that the division of the legislature would re-establish a privileged class in a society in which all men were now supposed to be equal. The Assembly decided instead to create a one-house legislature, free to act almost without restrictions because it directly represented the will of the people. The king was given only a suspensive veto—the right to delay legislation for three two-year sessions of the Assembly.

The October Days

Although he had appeared ready to bow to the power of the Revolution after the fall of the Bastille, Louis XVI resisted the drastic restructuring of government and society implied by the 4 August decrees and the Declaration of Rights. Throughout the month of September, the king refused to make a public statement accepting them. According to the principle of national sovereignty proclaimed by the Assembly, these decrees did not need the king's approval, but the deputies, having kept him on his throne, wanted his cooperation. Louis's foot-dragging raised public suspicions, not only among the deputies but also in the general population. In Paris, continuing high bread prices exacerbated discontent; the king was blamed for not alleviating the distress of his people.

When reports reached Paris that an army regiment recently summoned to Versailles had held a raucous banquet in which the patriotic tricolor cockade was supposedly trampled on the floor, popular anger exploded. The first to react were women, who connected the still-elevated price of bread to the counterrevolutionary atmosphere at the court. On 5 October, a large crowd of women assembled at the Hôtel de Ville to demand that the city government take action to protect the Revolution. They seized several cannon, and, accompanied by male members of the National Guard, set out to march on the royal palace at Versailles. The Guard commander Lafayette reluctantly accompanied the expedition to avoid losing control over his own troops.

The marchers reached the royal palace late at night. After bloody clashes that led to the killing of several palace guards, the king agreed to demands that he and his family should come to Paris; the National Assembly, relegated to the sidelines during the confrontation, had no choice but to agree to follow. On 6 October 1789, the royal family set off, accompanied by marchers who were carrying the severed heads of the royal guards on pikes and noisily celebrating their success in bringing "the baker, the baker's wife, and the baker's boy" (the king, queen, and their son) back to the city. Like the storming of the Bastille on 14 July, the "October Days" showed that popular violence could have major political effects: the king and the Assembly, brought to Paris by force, were now much more exposed to organized pressure from the populace. The uprising also demonstrated that women, normally excluded from politics, could play a decisive part in public events.

Once they had relocated to Paris, the deputies continued their work on the constitution. Deciding which citizens should have the right to vote proved to be another contentious issue. Most deputies accepted the argument that only citizens who owned a certain amount of property, and thus had something to lose from radical measures, could be expected to make intelligent political choices. In December 1789, they decided to restrict voting rights to "active" citizens, defined as adult males who paid taxes equivalent to three days of an ordinary laborer's wage and were not hired servants; the rest of the population were labeled "passive" citizens. There was an even higher wealth qualification for deputies. By the standards of the time, the property qualification for voting was quite modest, allowing well over half the adult male population to vote in national elections. The restriction on eligibility to the legislature was much tighter: only about 72,000 men, many of them nobles rather than bourgeois, met the qualifications. Defenders of these provisions were hard put to answer Robespierre's challenge, "Can the law be termed an expression of the general will when the greater number of those for whom it is made can have no hand in its making?"[2] In March 1790, the Assembly voted to let the colonies determine voting qualifications for themselves, allowing the white plantation owners who controlled politics there to exclude even the wealthy free people of color whose representatives had hoped the deputies would take up their cause.

Even though the Assembly barred the poorest citizens from any direct participation in politics, the deputies were concerned with the condition of the lower classes. The Assembly's Committee on the Needy made a full-scale inquiry into France's social problems and proposed that the government assume responsibility for supporting orphans, the poor, and the elderly. Access to "prompt, free, assured, and complete" medical care, it declared, was a basic human right. The new constitution included a mandate to make elementary education available to all citizens. Unfortunately, neither the National Assembly nor any subsequent revolutionary government ever found the resources to implement these sweeping proposals. Furthermore, some of the laws the Assembly passed did adversely affect the poorer classes. The Le Chapelier law of June 1791, for example, which barred all "coalitions" aimed at affecting wages and prices, made workers' organizations and strikes illegal and is frequently cited as evidence of the Assembly's dedication to bourgeois interests. On the other hand, however, the Assembly enacted some measures that ran contrary to the interests of important members of the bourgeoisie. In August 1790, it did away with the requirement that defendants in court cases be represented by lawyers, and a March 1791 law allowing all citizens to practice any profession led to the end of licensing for doctors. Anyone who wanted to could now practice law or medicine.

Ambivalent in its attitude toward economic inequality, the National Assembly gave clearer support to the extension of civil rights. French Protestants had already been granted limited rights in 1787. The Assembly, which included several Protestant deputies, quickly declared that they were now full citizens. The status of other minorities proved more controversial. Thanks to the efforts of deputies such as the abbé Grégoire, a Catholic priest who defended civil rights on religious grounds, the Assembly finally granted rights to all French Jews in one of its final sessions in September 1791. For the first time in Europe, non-Christians were made citizens. The legal system was reformed to abolish *lettres de cachet* and to give defendants a better chance of proving their innocence. The censorship system had collapsed in the summer of 1789; the Assembly debated several proposals to limit the "excesses" of the press, but in practice left it completely uncontrolled. In the fall of 1790, the Ogé rebellion, an uprising by free colored people in France's most important colony, Saint-Domingue, made the Assembly reconsider its stand on racial issues. In May 1791, it passed a decree granting full citizenship to nonwhite males born to free parents in the colonies. Even this limited concession was too much for the white population of the Caribbean colonies, but by the time their lobbyists had persuaded the Assembly to reverse its decision in September 1791, the great slave rebellion in Saint-Domingue that was to lead eventually to the abolition of slavery and the colony's independence had already broken out.

One of the Assembly's most enduring accomplishments was its division of France into new administrative districts called departments. These units, of approximately equal size and named after prominent geographic features such as rivers or mountains, were intended to rationalize France's administrative system and to break down loyalties to the old provinces that might conflict with commitment to the nation as a whole. The maps of the many overlapping court districts, religious dioceses, and other administrative divisions of the Old Regime were redrawn to correspond to departmental boundaries, which made citizens' relations with the government much simpler. With minor modifications, the departments created in 1789 have survived to the present day. Along with its redrawing of the administrative map, the Assembly abolished all the various tolls and customs boundaries that had divided France economically. The entire country thus became a unified market; the deputies assumed that this outcome would encourage manufacturing and commerce.

The decentralized system of local government initially set up in 1790 proved far less enduring than the creation of the departments and the elimination of trade barriers. Elected local officials were to collect taxes, administer justice, and enforce laws. The central government became almost totally dependent on the cooperation of these local authorities to carry out its directives and take on even unpopular duties such as collecting taxes. Before long, conflicts between local and national officials, as well as between the departments and local communities, proved that this system contained dangerous weaknesses. The redrawing of administrative boundaries also pitted towns against their neighbors, as each fought to capture as many government agencies for themselves as possible. Participation in this scramble was one of the ways in which local elites throughout the country learned the ropes of the new political culture.

The Expropriation of Church Lands and the Assignats

The liberal legislation enacted by the National Assembly had the potential to create a conflict between the wealthy bourgeoisie, who stood to benefit most from the new system, and the mass of the population: the Third Estate was no longer a united block. But the issue that most visibly threatened the liberal revolution grew out of the Assembly's attempt to reform the French Catholic Church.

The Assembly first faced this issue in November 1789, when it voted to expropriate the Church's property. Decades of denunciation of the clergy's mismanaged wealth had paved the way for this idea. Furthermore, since the Assembly intended to have the civil government take over many of the functions traditionally performed by the Church, such as schooling and aid to the poor, it seemed logical that the government should inherit the resources that the Church had used to pay for these services. Most important in the deputies' minds, however, was the idea that by selling off the Church lands, the government would be able to repay the massive debts left over from the Old Regime. As proponents of the measure pointed out, the purchasers of this property would acquire a vested interest in defending the Revolution. Opponents warned that if the government could confiscate the Church's property, it could eventually take over other citizens' goods as well. "We are attacked today...your turn will come," the abbé Maury told the nonreligious members of the Assembly.[3] But even many of the underpaid parish priests who were now to receive salaries from the state supported the move.

FIGURE 3.1 Provinces and Departments

The boundaries of France's prerevolutionary provinces kept alive memories of the long process by which the kingdom had been built up. The new departments, created in 1790, fostered a sense of national unity and also allowed for a more efficient system of administration.

Since the Church's landholdings were too extensive to be sold off all at once without flooding the market, the National Assembly issued certificates backed by the presumed value of the church lands, known as *assignats*, that could be redeemed for property when it came on the market. Government creditors were paid in assignats, which soon became a form of paper currency, used for ordinary business transactions and the payment of taxes. Initially, the quantity of this paper money in circulation was limited, and the bills were accepted at close to their face value. But when tax revenues fell short, successive revolutionary governments were constantly tempted to issue more of them. Eventually, the depreciation of the assignats became one of the Revolution's most pressing problems.

The expropriation of its property obligated the National Assembly to go further in restructuring the Church. In February 1790, the Assembly abolished monastic religious orders, except for those devoted to teaching and charitable activities. Monks and nuns were now free to renounce their vows and become ordinary citizens. More than the seizure of Church property, this measure overtly reflected Enlightenment hostility to religious beliefs. For many Catholics, the granting of full civil and political rights to religious minorities was a jarring change. In the southern city of Nîmes, where Catholics and Protestants had long been in conflict with each other, this change in the religious status quo led to bloody violence, and some Catholics came to regard the Revolution as a Protestant plot against their faith.

The Civil Constitution of the Clergy

Having deprived the Church of its property and its income from the tithe, the deputies had to find a new way of financing the institution. In July 1790, they enacted a set of laws known as the Civil Constitution of the Clergy that had much greater impact on the laity than their previous measures. Church reform had been a widespread demand throughout the eighteenth century, and numerous cahiers had encouraged the Estates-General to carry it out. Even most of the clergy recognized that major changes were long overdue. It was the nature of the reforms imposed and the lack of consultation with the Church that caused conflict.

The Civil Constitution redrew the boundaries of dioceses to correspond to the boundaries of the departments it had established, thereby abolishing more than one-third of the prerevolutionary bishoprics. More controversial was the decision to have departmental electoral assemblies choose curés and bishops. The French kings had long had the right to nominate bishops. Now that sovereignty was vested in the people rather than the king, it seemed logical to the legislators that this power should pass to the people's representatives. But the reform overturned the hierarchical structure of the Church, under which authority descended from God through the Pope to the bishops, who in turn consecrated priests. Devout Catholics objected that the assemblies charged with selecting priests might include Protestants, Jews, and atheists.

Most of the Assembly's members had little patience with these Catholic loyalists. Deputies who shared the Enlightenment's critical attitude toward the church were eager to remodel the institution. Others, though religious, were imbued with traditional Jansenist distrust of the Pope and the Church hierarchy. When many priests objected to the Civil Constitution of the Clergy, the Assembly decided to require those who wanted to keep their posts to take an oath of fidelity. This forced every French priest to make a public choice. To take the oath was to endorse the claim that the nation had authority over religious matters; to refuse it was to challenge that assertion. Slightly more than half of the parish clergy took the oath, but the remainder, including all but seven French bishops, refused. Where parish priests refused the oath, the government sought to install newly promoted priests who had accepted it, often in the face of violent local resistance to the "intruder" from laypeople who blamed the Revolution for destroying the "true" faith. The imposition of the Civil Constitution thus raised in acute form the issue of how far the revolutionary government could go in imposing its decisions on citizens who opposed them. The controversy caused by the Civil Constitution left the country deeply divided. Some modern historians, such as the American scholar Timothy Tackett, have claimed that this dispute, more than anything else, served to determine which regions would identify themselves with the revolutionary reforms and which would remain opposed to the new ideas for decades to come.

The growing controversy over the clergy's oath foreshadowed a major change in the course of the Revolution. For most of the twelve months following the storming of the Bastille, the movement had appeared to have overwhelming support. Opposition to it had come primarily from circles close to the Court and from some of the nobility, small groups associated with the most discredited aspects of the old society. The argument over Church reform proved different. For the first time, a significant part of the population, including large numbers of commoners, resisted a major piece of revolutionary legislation. Supporters of the Revolution now faced the question of how far they were prepared to go to impose their ideas on those members of the population who refused to accept them; its opponents were often driven to violence to resist the government.

Critical Thinking Questions

1. The Declaration of the Rights of Man and Citizen of 1789 was the most important summary of the basic principles behind the Revolution. Analyze the way in which the Declaration defined citizens' rights and tried to ensure that the government would respect them.
2. After passing the Declaration of Rights, the National Assembly established the basic features of France's new constitution. Explain the significance of the Assembly's decisions about the powers of the king, the nature of legislature, and the division of the country into new territorial units.
3. Among the National Assembly's most important initiatives was its attempt to reform the French Catholic Church. Discuss why the revolutionaries took on this challenge, and the consequences of the reforms they tried to make.

Notes

1. Cited in Guy Chaussinand-Nogaret, *Mirabeau* (Paris: Seuil, 1982), 224.
2. Cited in George Rudé, ed., *Robespierre* (Upper Saddle River, NJ: Prentice Hall, 1967), 14.
3. Cited in Florin Aftalion, *L'économie de la Révolution française* (Paris: Hachette, 1987), 91.

CHAPTER 4

The Defeat of the Liberal Revolution, 1790–1792

LEARNING OBJECTIVES

After studying this chapter, you will be able to:

- **Identify the major characteristics of the Revolution's new political culture.**
- **Explain the reasons for the king's flight to Varennes and its consequences.**
- **Discuss the impact of the Saint-Domingue uprising and the declaration of war against Austria on the French Revolution.**
- **Discuss the nature of the "second Revolution" of 10 August 1792 and its implications.**

A crowd of 300,000 attended the Festival of the Federation held in Paris on 14 July 1790 to commemorate the first anniversary of the storming of the Bastille. The celebration began in pouring rain. As the ceremonies proceeded, however, the sun broke through the clouds. Participants saw it as a good omen: perhaps the difficulties besetting the first stages of the Revolution would also blow over. Instead, however, the conflicts inspired by the radical effort to remake French society became more intense. The deputies to the National Assembly hoped that the completion of the new constitution in September 1791 would put an end to these disputes. By the time they finished their work, however, it was already clear that there would be continuing resistance to many parts of it, both from conservatives who opposed to the Revolution and from groups who claimed that the new laws did not fulfill the promises made in the Declaration of Rights. All sides were increasingly willing to resort to violence to defeat their enemies. In April 1792, the violence of an international war was added to the nation's domestic conflicts, and four months later, a violent revolutionary insurrection, the *journée* of 10 August 1792, ended both the French monarchy and the liberal phase of the Revolution.

The New Political Culture

One reason for France's continuing instability was the growth of a new political culture that made it possible for almost all of the population to express its views. The political institutions established by the National Assembly were meant to limit participation to "active" citizens, the wealthier male members of the national community, but the informal institutions of revolutionary political culture were more accessible. Three fundamental features of this new political culture were newspapers, political clubs, and public festivals. Anyone could read a newspaper or hear it read aloud; club meetings were frequently open to the poor and to women, and even children participated in festivals. There was thus from the start a potential conflict between the constitution-makers' efforts to limit political participation and the openness embodied in these informal institutions.

The periodical press allowed the public to follow the proceedings of the National Assembly and the other events of the Revolution, and to voice their own opinions. As soon as the Estates-General convened, the monarchy's censorship system broke down. Over 130 new journals were launched before the end of 1789. Circulating throughout the country, these periodicals allowed readers all over the country to follow the Revolution as it unfolded and thus created a sense of national community. The press was one of the first professions in which the revolutionary promise of "careers open to talent" was fully realized. If readers responded to their words, previously unknown writers could quickly establish themselves as national political figures. Radical revolutionaries such as Camille Desmoulins, a young lawyer who had helped launch the mobilization that led to the storming of the Bastille, and Jean-Paul Marat, an eccentric doctor and scientist who styled himself as *L'Ami du peuple* ("The Friend of the People"), quickly became powers to be reckoned with. Counterrevolutionary polemicists used the press just as effectively as did advocates of change. Extremist writers, such as Marat and some of his royalist counterparts, openly encouraged violence, even calling for the killing of the deputies of the National Assembly.

Clubs channeled and organized the public's participation in the new politics. The first ones grew out of the informal gatherings in coffeehouses and other public places that had accompanied the elections to the Estates-General. By November 1789, a group of Patriot deputies had founded a club that met regularly to plan common strategy in the Assembly. The club soon expanded to include private citizens as well as legislators and named itself the *Society of Friends of the Constitution,* but it was more commonly referred to as the Jacobin Club, because it met in a church formerly owned by the Jacobin order. Provincial supporters of the Revolution formed clubs that affiliated with the Jacobins in Paris. By mid-1791, there were 434 Jacobin clubs, and the number grew into the thousands during the Revolution's radical phase in 1793–1794. These clubs brought supporters of the Revolution together to hear the latest news from the Assembly, discuss the issues of the day, and plan local political initiatives. At first, membership in the Jacobins was restricted by a relatively high admission fee, and the early Jacobins tended to be substantial members of the middle classes who distrusted radicalism. In later years, however, membership in the Jacobins was opened up to poorer citizens, and the club network supported increasingly radical policies.

The Jacobins' national network gave them a unique importance, but there were numerous other political clubs, particularly in Paris. Radical revolutionaries including the journalists Desmoulins and Marat and the future popular leader Georges Danton led the Cordeliers Club, which welcomed disenfranchised "passive" citizens and campaigned against what it saw as the National Assembly's bias in favor of the rich. Women, although excluded from the electoral politics of the Revolution, participated in many of the clubs, such as the *Cercle social*, founded by Parisian supporters of political and religious democracy. Women also formed their own clubs in at least sixty provincial towns. Counterrevolutionaries had their own groupings, such as the *Club Massiac*, formed by representatives of the plantation owners in France's Caribbean colonies to defend slavery. Patriot hostility obstructed the spread of counterrevolutionary groups, however; in some instances, violent demonstrations broke up their meetings.

Public festivals provided a symbolic representation of the Revolution's achievements in which the entire population could participate. The first of these celebrations were largely spontaneous, like the planting of "liberty trees"—poles festooned with revolutionary symbols—in many towns in early 1790. In the spring of that year, local patriotic groups and units of the National Guard began organizing "federations," bringing together groups from several towns or regions for ceremonies honoring the new constitution. This movement culminated on 14 July 1790 in the national Festival of Federation celebrated on Paris's Champ de Mars, now the site of the Eiffel Tower. Before an enormous crowd, the King and the leaders of the Assembly and the National Guard swore loyalty to the new constitution. Press reports and the accounts of those who had come from the provinces gave the entire country a sense of having taken part. The same impulse that inspired festivals also drove the revolutionaries to create more permanent monuments to the movement. When the Patriot leader Mirabeau died in April 1791, the National Assembly voted to transform the Church of Saint Geneviève into the Pantheon, a memorial to the country's "great men." The transfer of Voltaire's remains to the Pantheon in July 1791 was marked by another large festival, which emphasized the Revolution's roots in the Enlightenment and its increasing separation from the Church, which had denied the free-thinking *philosophe* a public funeral at his death in 1778.

The King's Flight and the Crisis of 1791

The growing number of people who followed political events and wanted to influence them made it difficult to confine conflicts to the Assembly in Paris. As the National Assembly tried to impose the Civil Constitution of the Clergy on reluctant "refractory" priests and their congregations in the fall of 1790, local incidents of opposition multiplied. This religious conflict led directly to the undermining of the National Assembly's constitutional system because it helped drive Louis XVI to make an open break with the Assembly in June 1791. A devout Catholic, the king was deeply troubled when the Pope condemned the Civil Constitution of the Clergy in March 1791, after Louis XVI had signed it into law. The king was also under pressure in early 1791 because he had refused Assembly demands for strong measures against the nobles and members of the royal family who fled abroad after July 1789. From their refuges in the small German principalities along the Rhine, these *émigrés* sought to organize an army to invade France. They also lobbied foreign powers to invade France and free the king. Louis issued appeals to his relatives but failed to convince either the émigrés or the supporters of the Revolution that he meant them. In addition, the king feared for his own safety and that of his family, particularly after a Paris crowd physically prevented them from leaving the palace to attend Easter church services in the nearby town of Saint-Cloud in April 1791.

On the night of 20 June 1791, the king finally tried to get out of his increasingly awkward situation by fleeing from Paris. By the time the king's disappearance was discovered the next morning, he and his family had already escaped from the capital. A nervous National Assembly immediately sent couriers in pursuit while announcing to the public that the monarch had been "abducted." The discovery that Louis had left behind a manifesto denouncing the Revolution discredited this story, but the Assembly hesitated to condemn the king and to commit itself to replacing him: the entire constitutional edifice so painfully erected since July 1789 would be called into question. Bad luck and the king's chronic indecisiveness foiled the royal family's plan. Their large and conspicuous stagecoach attracted attention along the road, and delays caused them to miss their rendezvous with loyal troops who had been recruited to escort them. In the small town of Varennes, near the northern frontier, the fugitives were recognized and arrested by the local authorities. Heavily guarded, the royal party traveled back to Paris.

The king's flight to Varennes forced supporters of the Revolution to consider the possibility that France might be better off without a monarch. The Cordeliers Club urged the National Assembly "in the name of the fatherland, to declare immediately that France is no longer a monarchy...," and much of the population seemed ready to accept the idea of a republican government, in which all political leaders would be chosen by the people. The leaders of the National Assembly quickly decided, however, that they needed to preserve the monarchy in spite of the king. Barnave, one of the most eloquent spokesmen for the Third Estate in June 1789, now became the main defender of this policy. He spoke for many who had supported the Revolution's assault on noble privileges but were now alarmed by the success of radicals who denounced the unequal distribution of wealth and property and called for stronger measures against the Revolution's opponents. If France was to become a stable country in which the rights of property owners were secure, Barnave argued, there had to be a strong executive authority, independent of public opinion, to maintain the laws. To remove the king from office would be to "begin the Revolution anew" and to invite demands for complete democracy and the redistribution of property. (See Document E.)

Barnave and his followers prevailed in the National Assembly, which voted to absolve the king for his flight if he would swear an oath to the new constitution, but they also split the revolutionary movement. On 16 July 1791, Barnave and most of the other deputies quit the Jacobin Club, leaving behind a small rump organization led by Robespierre, and founded a rival club, the Feuillants. On the following day, Paris radicals called for a mass demonstration to sign a petition protesting the Assembly's decision. Although the protesters were largely peaceful, the National Guard commander, Lafayette, and the mayor of Paris, Bailly, both sympathetic to the Feuillants, seized an isolated incident of violence as a pretext to send in the National Guard. About sixty demonstrators were shot down in the ensuing "massacre of the Champ-de-Mars," making it the worst incident of bloodshed in the city since the storming of the Bastille. This repression appeared to confirm the radical claim that the Assembly despised the common people. A constitution put into effect under these conditions rested on shaky foundations.

The End of the National Assembly

With the king's fate resolved and the radicals temporarily silent, the National Assembly hastened to conclude its work. In August and September 1791, the deputies "revised" the entire constitution, altering a number of clauses to strengthen safeguards for property owners. The conflict over the Civil Constitution of the Clergy, the king's flight, and the massacre of 17 July 1791 showed that grave difficulties threatened the new liberal order, but the deputies could be forgiven for taking pride in what they had accomplished. They had broken the political deadlock that had prevented necessary political reforms for decades. They had given France a complete new constitutional system, based on the principles of legal equality for all male citizens and individual liberty. If they failed to solve some of the most pressing problems they had come up against, such as poverty and education, they had at least proclaimed principles that, a century or more later, would become the basis for effective legislation.

Critics at the time and since have blamed the National Assembly for trying to do too much too quickly and for failing to provide sufficient checks and balances in their constitutional system. As early as February 1790, an English observer, Edmund Burke, had published a scathing indictment of the entire revolutionary enterprise.

DOCUMENT E

Three Reactions to the King's Flight

These three excerpts from the Paris press show how the king's attempted flight in June 1791 divided the country. A royalist writer applauded the king for his action.

"I salute you, king of the French. I won't call it a crime for you to have tried to recapture the scepter you inherited from your noble ancestors. The attempt you have just made to break your chains enhances your standing in the eyes of all the French." (*Journal général de la cour et de la ville,* 28 June 1791)

The *Gazette universelle*, a newspaper subsidized by members of the politically moderate Feuillant club, argued that the king needed to be kept on the throne for the good of the nation.

"It is not for Louis XVI that the monarchy has been established... It is to counterbalance the weight of a single legislative body; it is to prevent a perpetual clash of private ambitions striving for the highest post; it is to assure the separation of powers, without which there is neither liberty nor constitution; it is to maintain the indivisibility of the empire, without which we are at the mercy of any ambitious neighbor." (*Gazette universelle,* 10 July 1791)

The radical journalist Jean-Paul Marat, the "Friend of the People," directed his fury at the legislators who had refused to punish the king.

"May this horrible crime against the sovereignty of the people be the last one. May the Parisians finally open their eyes, and realize that the moment has come to get rid of this infamous assembly which has sold out the rights and the interests of the nation for so long... " [France's provinces should] "form a just and free government among themselves.... May they be virtuous enough to establish a pure democracy."

(*L'Ami du peuple*, 15 July 1791) (Translations by Jeremy D. Popkin.)

"You began ill, because you began by despising every thing that belonged to you. You set up your trade without a capital," Burke warned the French, arguing that historic tradition was a better guide for political reform than the abstract principles to which the National Assembly had appealed. He predicted that the expropriation of Church lands would lead to a general attack on property and that the weakening of the king's power would ultimately lead to the complete demise of the monarchy. Burke's eloquent denunciation of the Revolution and his defense of tradition made him the first great spokesman for conservatism, the principled opposition to sudden and thoroughgoing social and political change.

Burke was one of the few foreign observers to take such a negative view of the movement in its early phases. News of the dramatic events in France attracted visitors from all over the world who wanted to see the great political experiment for themselves, and many of them became enthusiastic propagandists for the movement. The Anglo-American Thomas Paine, whose pamphlets had helped inspire the American movement for independence, moved to France and wrote a best-selling reply to Burke, *The Rights of Man,* and the published letters of Helen Maria Williams, a friend of the women's rights pioneer Mary Wollstonecraft, gave readers a pro-revolutionary account of events in Paris. Wollstonecraft herself joined Williams there in 1792. Americans were especially enthusiastic, seeing the French Revolution as an extension of their own movement. The French "appear to have been destined to give lessons to the world by the wisdom of their new institutions," an American poet, Joel Barlow, wrote after a stay in Paris in 1791, and Thomas Jefferson "consider[ed] the establishment and success of their government as necessary to stay up our own."[1]

The Legislative Assembly

The election procedures set up in the constitution were unfamiliar and cumbersome, and so fewer than 25 percent of the "active" citizens entitled to vote under the new constitution actually did so in 1791. The 745 deputies they elected were all newcomers to national politics: in May 1791, Robespierre had embarrassed the National Assembly into adopting a "self-denying ordinance" forbidding its own members to seek election to the new legislature they were designing. Most of the deputies who assembled for the first time on 1 October 1791 were from the bourgeois groups that had gained the most from the National Assembly's reforms. Many had served as local officials and had had to deal with refractory priests and other opponents of the Revolution. Determined to ensure the triumph of the movement, they nevertheless remained concerned about protecting social order and the rights of property.

At the outset, the moderate Feuillant group, formed after the king's flight to Varennes and dedicated to making the new constitutional system work, had more supporters in the new assembly than the radical Jacobins. Outside the Legislative Assembly, however, the more radical revolutionaries had managed to hold the loyalty of most of the provincial club network, giving them a powerful propaganda tool, and the Jacobins soon gained the initiative over their rivals. The radicals also had support in the Paris population, particularly from groups like the Cordeliers Club, whose members advocated political rights for the common people.

While the radicals pressured the Legislative Assembly from the left, the deputies also had to contend with counterrevolutionary agitation from the right. There were no openly declared counterrevolutionary deputies in the Legislative Assembly, but outspoken royalist journalists kept up a vociferous campaign for the overthrow of the new constitution. They criticized the king for his apparent willingness to accept the role of a constitutional monarch, openly urged army officers to emigrate and take up arms against the Revolution, and called for a foreign invasion to quash the movement. "Refractory" priests who had refused to accept the Civil Constitution of the Clergy often became rallying points for local resistance to the Revolution in the provinces, where they found strong support among devout women churchgoers.

In this tense atmosphere, the Legislative Assembly continued to work on the details of legislation to fit the new constitution. Its members continued the National Assembly's efforts to create a society of independent individuals with equal rights. For example, the Legislative Assembly completed the secularization of identity by making the registration of births, marriages, and deaths—known in France as the *état civil*—a function of the government rather than the Church. The new legislation authorized divorce and allowed husbands and wives equal rights to initiate proceedings. Divorces could be granted not just for adultery and other violations of the marriage contract, but also on the basis of mutual consent or "incompatibility of temperament." This reform made marriage a voluntary agreement between consenting adults, just as the revolutionary legislators claimed that society was the result of a voluntary agreement among all citizens. A law regulating inheritance guaranteed daughters portions of their parents' estate equal to those given to sons. Even as they gave women increased rights within the family, however, the legislators rejected suggestions that they should be allowed to vote or hold office. (See Document F.) As part of the abolition of laws rooted in religious tradition, the Assembly also eliminated penalties for homosexual acts.

The Revolt in the Colonies and Unrest at Home

The increasingly agitated political atmosphere diverted most of the Legislative Assembly's attention to immediate threats to the Revolution, however. These threats included troubles in the colonies, domestic social unrest, and the threat of war. News of a massive slave revolt in France's most important colony, the Caribbean sugar island of Saint-Domingue, reached Paris in October 1791, two months after the insurrection had begun. Through contacts with sailors and domestic servants whose masters discussed the news from France, some slaves had heard rumors about the movement for liberty that had begun in 1789. They were also inspired by the example of earlier slave resistance movements, such as the Makandal conspiracy of 1757, which had spread fear throughout the colony's white population. The black insurgents burned crops and plantation buildings and massacred some slaveowners, although the number of blacks killed by whites far exceeded the victims of these attacks, a fact ignored in the lurid reports of violence that quickly spread throughout the Atlantic world. The upheaval in the colony had immediate effects on trade. Merchants demanded that the government take action to restore order, but antislavery spokesmen opposed sending troops unless the white plantation owners agreed to recognize the rights of the free colored population.

THE SAINT-DOMINGUE SLAVE INSURRECTION

Reports about the violent slave uprising in Saint-Domingue in August 1791 inspired this engraving showing whites being assaulted and plantations being set on fire. It is unlikely that the artist had ever actually seen the colonies, but such images contributed to the general atmosphere of violence in France itself. Modern historians usually conclude that the cruelty of slavery justified the means used to overthrow it.

The Legislative Assembly had to cope with spreading unrest closer to home as well. The 1791 grain harvest was a poor one, and by the fall, there were outbreaks of peasant violence in a number of rural areas. In February 1792, crowds in Paris, angered by the high price of sugar resulting from the disruption of production in Saint-Domingue, attacked merchants' shops. The deputies, who saw the Revolution as a movement on behalf of the people, could not understand why ordinary men and women would blame the movement for their economic problems. They found it easier to believe that members of the former privileged orders had incited these disturbances. Although the deputies supported a political system based on individual rights, many of them were now ready to back laws curtailing the rights of groups blamed for obstructing the new order. In November 1791, the Legislative Assembly voted stringent laws against refractory priests. Another law ordered émigré nobles to either return by the end of 1791 or face the loss of their

DOCUMENT F

Olympe De Gouges's Declaration of the Rights of Women Citizens, 1791

Olympe de Gouges, an independent-minded woman playwright, showed how the language of the Declaration of the Rights of Man could be appropriated to make a case for equal rights for women. Men at the time rejected her ideas as absurd, and her decision to speak out in defense of the king at the time of his trial in 1793 led to her arrest and execution during the Terror. Today, she is recognized as one of the founding figures of modern feminist thought.

"Considering that ignorance, forgetfulness, or contempt for the rights of woman are the sole causes of public misfortunes and the corruption of governments...the sex that is superior in beauty and in courage, by bearing the pains of childbirth, recognizes and declares, in the presence and under the protection of the Supreme Being, the following rights of Woman and Citizen: (1) Woman is born and remains equal to man in rights...(2) The purpose of all political associations is the protection of the natural and imprescriptible rights of Woman and Man...(4) the exercise of the natural rights of woman is only limited by the unending tyranny that man imposes on her; these limits should be redefined according to the laws of nature and of reason...(10) Woman has the right to mount the scaffold; she should have an equal right to mount the tribune...(13) Taxes are equal for women and men; she does her part of all obligatory work and all difficult tasks; she should have the same share of public appointments, positions, jobs, honors..."

(Translation by Jeremy D. Popkin.)

property and execution if they re-entered the country later. Louis XVI vetoed both these laws. His actions increased doubts about his loyalty to the new constitution.

The Move toward War

The issue of the émigrés was one of the main factors that drove the Legislative Assembly to its most important decision: its vote on 20 April 1792 to declare war against Austria. The revolutionaries of 1789 had been persuaded that war, the result of kings' greed for conquests and glory, was one of those evils of the Old Regime that they could abolish. In May 1790, when an incident in Nootka Sound in the northern Pacific led Spain to appeal for French support against England under a treaty between the two Bourbon monarchies, the National Assembly stripped the king of his traditional right to declare war. The Constitution of 1791 announced that "the French nation will never undertake any war of conquest, and will never employ its forces against the liberty of another people." The deputies warned, however, that the entire population would rise up if the country was attacked; war would no longer be a matter that only concerned the king. And even as France's new government promised an era of peace, it continued to push the costly program of naval expansion begun under the monarchy and intended to give the country a stronger position in any future war with Britain.

Despite the Assembly's renunciation of conquests, France's neighbors realized that the Revolution affected them. The principles contained in the Declaration of the Rights of Man and Citizen suggested that only governments that truly represented their nations were legitimate; they thus challenged the bases of absolute monarchy and social privilege, not just in France, but everywhere in Europe. Spain banned the circulation of news from France in December 1789, to protect its king's subjects from the bad example of their neighbor's revolt. More concretely, the National Assembly's insistence that all people had the right to choose their own government affected foreign rulers who claimed lands surrounded by French territory. Events in Avignon, a territory in southern France belonging to the Pope, showed how explosive this notion was. In June 1790, local revolutionaries overthrew the Papal government and demanded to be annexed to France. Cautious at first about supporting any group that threw off its old ruler and voted to join France, the National Assembly finally took the plunge in September 1791. Although the territory involved was small, the arguments used to justify this annexation had the potential to upset the entire traditional European order.

Initially, most of Europe's other governments had shown little hostility to the Revolution. Some assumed that the Revolution would weaken France's power and give them a free hand to pursue their own interests elsewhere. Prussia, Russia, and Austria, for example, turned their attention to blocking efforts at national reform in Poland, where a liberal constitution similar to the new French one was proclaimed in May 1791. Louis XVI's flight to Varennes finally led Leopold II of Austria, brother of Marie-Antoinette, and Frederic William II of Prussia to make a verbal gesture of support for him. The two rulers met in Pillnitz in August 1791 and issued a declaration suggesting possible intervention to restore the French king's authority.[2] This fueled French patriots' contention that the Revolution was in danger from abroad. When the plantation owners in Saint-Domingue appealed to nearby British and Spanish colonies for aid against the slave insurrection, revolutionaries saw additional evidence of foreign meddling in French affairs. The presence of French émigrés in territories in Austria's sphere of influence that were close to France's borders provided another pretext for denouncing foreign hostility.

In France, support for war came from the extremes of right and left. The Feuillant moderates opposed the idea, fearful that the fragile constitutional monarchy would not survive such an ordeal, but a majority of the radical Jacobin supporters of the Revolution openly favored hostilities. The leaders of the pro-war faction in the Jacobin Club came to be known as the Girondins, because many of their most prominent members were deputies from the Gironde, the department of Bordeaux. Their main spokesman was the journalist-deputy Jacques-Pierre Brissot; behind the scenes, they were influenced by Madame Roland, the spirited wife of another leading member, in whose salon the Girondin deputies regularly met. The Girondins tended to be talented and ambitious individualists who had made their way in the world thanks to their own abilities. No friends of the Old Regime, they advocated strong measures against counterrevolutionaries, but were nevertheless susceptible to the concerns of France's bourgeois elites; many of them represented the country's big trading cities, such as Bordeaux and Marseille.

The Girondins' leading spokesman Brissot argued that war would exalt patriotic fervor and expose traitors who hoped for the defeat of the Revolution. Furthermore, the radicals were confident that, as soon as French troops crossed their borders, the populations of neighboring countries would embrace the revolutionary cause and rise up against their own rulers. "Volcanoes are ready everywhere... it will only take a spark to start a universal explosion," Brissot promised.[3] Fearing that war would give the king a chance to recover his authority, Robespierre warned the Jacobins that "no one loves armed missionaries," but he was drowned out by Brissot's supporters.

The Jacobin war party found unlikely allies among the king's closest supporters. Once war was declared, these royalists thought, the king, as commander-in-chief of the army, would have expanded powers. If France was successful, his position would be strengthened; if the French army was defeated, the foreign powers would do away with the revolutionaries. The king himself had private doubts about the wisdom of these arguments, but in the end, he went along with them. On 10 March 1792, he appointed a new team of ministers close to the pro-war Girondin group: Madame Roland's husband became Interior Minister and a fiercely anti-Austrian general, Dumouriez, took over management of foreign affairs. When the Austrian government rejected a French ultimatum to expel the émigrés from German territory, the king asked the Assembly to declare war; and so, on 20 April 1792, France entered into a conflict that would last, with brief interruptions, for more than two decades.

The Impact of War

The declaration of war had an immediate and long-lasting impact on the course of the Revolution. It raised the stakes of political debate enormously. For patriots, opposition to any aspect of the Revolution now looked like treason and merited the harshest possible punishment. Political disputes now took on a life-or-death character that made compromise harder than ever to accept. The war also marked a further step in the political mobilization of the common people. As members of the lower classes were called on to fight, the constitutional exclusion of these "passive citizens" from full political rights became harder to justify.

The outbreak of war focused attention on the condition of the French army and navy. Until July 1789, the armed forces had been the king's, not the nation's. The army consisted primarily of long-term professional soldiers, many of them recruited from abroad. The officer corps was overwhelmingly aristocratic; regardless of merit, rank-and-file soldiers and sailors could not hope to rise above the rank of noncommissioned officers. The National Assembly had undertaken to reform the military, like every other French institution. Soldiers and sailors were given the same rights as other citizens, and recruitment for the officer corps was opened to commoners. New army units, composed of pro-revolutionary volunteers drawn from the National Guard, were created alongside the old "line" regiments, whose political attitudes were often suspect. By 1792, these reforms had been only partially successful. Many aristocratic officers' loyalty to the new revolutionary order was less than certain, and relations between the officers and their men were strained, as a bloody soldiers' revolt at Nancy in August 1790 and naval mutinies in the port of Brest in October 1790 and in Saint-Domingue had shown. At the start of the war, army morale was low. The troops were quick to blame their commanders for any reverses they suffered; at Lille, panicked French soldiers massacred their own commander. In Paris, news of these defeats plunged the institutions of the constitutional monarchy into a fatal crisis.

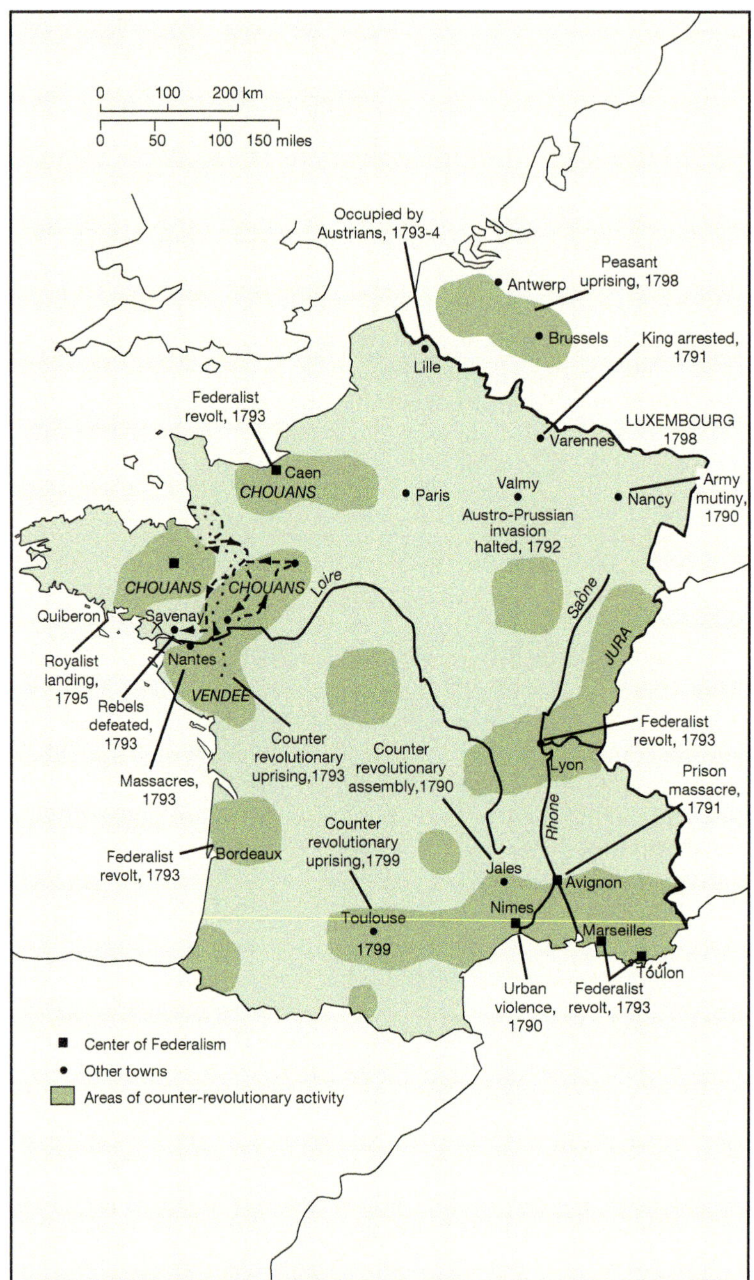

FIGURE 4.1 The Revolution in the Provinces

Events in the provinces had a major impact on the direction of the Revolution. The "Great Fear," the Nancy army mutiny, the king's flight to Varennes, the Vendée revolt, and the federalist uprisings all posed major crises for the revolutionary government in the capital.

The Overthrow of the Monarchy

By the start of the war, the constitutional system put into effect in 1791 was already coming apart. Particularly in Paris, the large population of artisans and shopkeepers who had made up most of the crowd that stormed the Bastille had never accepted their exclusion from politics. In the spring of 1792, pro-revolutionary political activists had mobilized strong support among these *sans-culottes,* so called to distinguish them from the educated classes, who wore elegant knee-breeches, or *culottes,* not the worker's long trousers. Sans-culotte activists began to mobilize against both the king and an Assembly that continued to dither as the Austro-Prussian army advanced into France. Alongside the sans-culottes, a small but determined group of women also made their presence felt, participating in street demonstrations and even demanding the right to bear arms, as male citizens did.

By the summer of 1792, activists from the popular movement had gained control of many of the forty-eight sections into which Paris had been divided in 1790. Even though voting in the sections' political assemblies and participation in their National Guard units were theoretically limited to "active" citizens, by the summer of 1792, many poorer members of the population refused to accept this exclusion. The growing strength of this popular movement became visible on 20 June 1792, when a sans-culotte crowd invaded the royal palace to protest the king's veto of several measures aimed at strengthening the war effort. The Jacobin deputies kept their distance from this protest, whose organizers came primarily from the radical Cordeliers Club, but they shared the crowd's fear that the king was deliberately dragging his feet to give the Austro-Prussian invaders time to reach Paris. Agitation was not confined to the capital: in many areas of the countryside, peasants demanded an end to the compensation payments they were supposed to make in exchange for the abolition of seigneurial dues.

At the beginning of July 1792, a small group of revolutionary militants in Paris, including radical journalists and sans-culotte leaders, drew up a plan to provoke an uprising to force the removal of the king and the summoning of a National Convention which would take emergency measures to defend the country and give France a new constitution. In addition to the armed battalions of the more radical Paris sections, the plotters relied on the armed *fédérés,* volunteer units from all over the country that had come to Paris for the celebration of 14 July. The unit from Marseille was especially noted for its revolutionary ardor. Its members had arrived in Paris singing a new marching song composed a few months earlier whose verses called on all "children of the Fatherland" to take arms and let "the blood of our enemies water our fields." This "song of the Marseillais" became a rallying cry for the assault on the monarchy.

On 28 July 1792, the commander of the allied forces, the Duke of Brunswick, issued a proclamation holding the inhabitants of Paris responsible for any attack on the king. When the news of this "Brunswick manifesto" reached Paris, the insurrectionary leaders decided to act. By 9:00 A.M. on 10 August, thousands of their supporters were converging on the Tuileries. The king and his family took refuge with the Legislative Assembly, leaving their loyal Swiss guards behind to defend the

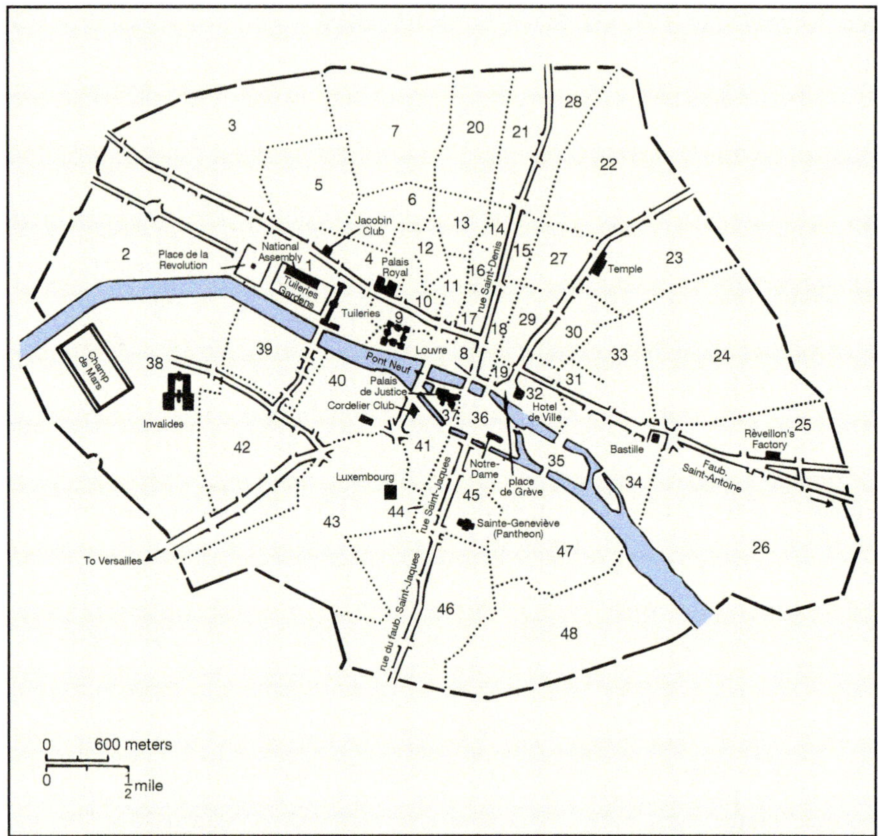

FIGURE 4.2 Revolutionary Paris

The revolutionary legislatures occupied buildings near the old royal palaces, the Louvre and the Tuileries, in the center of the city. The Hôtel-de-Ville, seat of Paris's municipal government, was closer to the eastern faubourgs, home of the sans-culotte militants whose organized marches put pressure on the government at many critical moments during the Revolution. Dotted lines show the boundaries of the forty-eight sections into which the city was divided after 1790.

palace. In the course of the day, fighting broke out; the outnumbered guards killed at least 100 of the insurgents. This action infuriated the sans-culottes, who retaliated by massacring the guards who fell into their hands. The tenth of August thus became by far the bloodiest of the revolutionary insurrections, or *journées*. It was also among the most decisive politically. The Legislative Assembly suspended Louis XVI from his functions and voted to call nationwide elections for a Convention that would determine the fate of the monarchy; it thus scrapped the Constitution of 1791. By declaring that all adult males were eligible to vote for the Convention, the Assembly abandoned the effort to keep power in the hands of the propertied classes. The liberal or bourgeois Revolution had ended; the democratic and radical Revolution had begun.

Emergency Measures and Revolutionary Government

The six weeks between the uprising of 10 August and the first session of the National Convention gave France its first taste of what came to be called revolutionary government, as ordinary legal processes were suspended in the name of defending the Revolution. During this period, control of Paris was shared uneasily by the Legislative Assembly—half of whose members had ceased to attend meetings after the uprising—and the municipal assembly, called the Commune, whose members included sans-culotte militants and Jacobin radicals such as Robespierre. The most visible figure during this crisis was a veteran member of the radical Cordeliers Club, Georges Danton. A fiery speaker with a gift for communicating with the common people, Danton had played a key role in the sans-culotte capture of the Paris sections (neighborhood assemblies) before the uprising. Named minister of justice after 10 August, he pushed his colleagues to satisfy radical demands for fast action. "We must dare, and dare again, and dare forever, and so France will be saved!" he proclaimed. To satisfy the popular pressure for action, the Legislative Assembly set up a Revolutionary Tribunal on 17 August 1792. Its procedures superseded many of the guarantees in the Declaration of the Rights of Man. There was no appeal from its sentences, and those condemned to death were executed with a new mechanical beheading device that experts had created for the National Assembly, which was supposed to be painless and efficient—the guillotine, named for Dr. Guillotin, a legislator who had wanted to abolish cruel punishments. Other emergency measures included the deportation of "refractory" priests and the dispatch of commissioners to the provinces to bring local governments in line with the new situation in Paris. In an attempt to pacify the peasants, the Legislative Assembly ended almost all reimbursement payments to former seigneurs.

These actions were not enough to satisfy the sans-culottes' demand for immediate measures to defeat the counterrevolution, however. On 2 September 1792, reacting to news that the key fortress of Verdun was about to surrender, sans-culotte militants surrounded the principal Paris prisons. They set up improvised tribunals and forced the jailers to bring out the prisoners. In all, some 1,300 people, most of them guilty of nothing more tangible than having held privileged status before 1789, were killed. The massacres continued for several days, and neither the Legislative Assembly nor the Commune made any effort to stop them. These killings stained the Revolution's reputation throughout Europe; they also made the incoming Convention acutely aware of the need to convince the sans-culottes that it was doing everything necessary to defend the Revolution, in order to keep them from resorting to violent action.

In the aftermath of the September massacres, the Revolution's destiny depended on the outcome of the Austro-Prussian invasion. On 20 September 1792, the day the Convention first assembled in Paris, the issue was settled by the battle of Valmy. The French, now better organized than in the first battles of the war, used their superiority in numbers and artillery to halt the Austro-Prussian advance. When Austrian officers sent to negotiate an armistice after the battle expressed surprise at how well the untrained citizen-soldiers had fought, a French officer proudly replied, "The French are all determined to be buried under the smoking ruins of their territory rather than give up their independence." The

THE SEPTEMBER MASSACRES IN PARIS

As foreign troops invaded France in 1792, revolutionary militants in Paris reacted by massacring some 1300 prisoners in the city's jails. The provisional government created after the uprising of 10 August 1792 did nothing to stop the violence. These "September massacres" are still the most controversial episode of violence in the whole Revolution.

invaders' decision to retreat and resume operations in the spring gave the radical revolutionary government precious time to consolidate its position.

The Failure of the Liberal Revolution

Was the collapse of the constitutional monarchy inevitable? If so, why? Critics have pointed to some shortcomings in the design of the 1791 constitution that helped hasten its demise. The logic of national sovereignty may have favored the idea of a one-house legislature, but practical experience in France and elsewhere has suggested that a bicameral system provides for greater stability. Giving the king the power to delay legislation with the suspensive veto but not to reject it altogether made him the target of protests if he opposed popular proposals, but it didn't give him real authority to defend his point of view. Even so, the internal flaws of the constitution were not so serious as to make it unworkable. Experience in a number of European countries during the nineteenth century demonstrated that constitutional monarchy could be a successful form of government, capable of evolving in the direction of fuller democracy.

In 1791, however, the French attempted to install a constitutional monarchy with a king who had proven his ill will toward such a system and with a legislature bent on enforcing controversial policies such as the Civil Constitution of the Clergy. At the same time, the king and the new assembly had to face a growing challenge from below to the principle of limiting political rights to the propertied classes. There was also a vocal counterrevolutionary opposition that openly sought to destroy the new institutions. In addition to all these internal difficulties, the new government had to contend with a dangerous international environment.

The absence of consensus about how to deal with these problems certainly undermined the new political system.

Historians in the republican and Marxist traditions, such as Georges Lefebvre, see the disintegration of the constitutional monarchy and the "second revolution" of 1792 as a logical continuation of the original Revolution of 1789. By proclaiming the principle of popular sovereignty, the original revolutionaries had fatally undermined hereditary authority. The principle of equality discredited their own effort to limit political rights to property owners, and the peasants had never accepted the idea that they should have to pay for the abolition of burdens inherited from what the revolutionaries themselves called an unjust regime. For these historians, it was inevitable that the common people would demand a system of government that truly represented their will, and the violence that accompanied these demands was necessary to overcome opposition. All historians recognize, however, that the decision to go to war in April 1792 changed the character of the Revolution, greatly accelerating the move toward radicalism. Some scholars see this outcome as evidence that the Revolution had "deviated" from its original path. Many of them also stress that the "second revolution" was never a true mass movement. The Jacobins and the sans-culotte movement represented organized minorities, and in the countryside, many areas were clearly hostile or indifferent to the new revolutionary radicalism. Although historians generally agree that the constitutional monarchy set up in 1791 had little chance of success, debate continues about the nature of the forces that destroyed it.

Critical Thinking Questions

1. The French Revolution created a new political culture, quite different from that of the absolute monarchy it overthrew. Explain how this new political culture reflected the ideas of liberty and equality embodied in the Declaration of the Rights of Man. What new forms of political instability did this democratic political culture create?
2. In June 1791, Louis XVI and his family attempted to flee Paris. Why did the king's action create a crisis for the revolutionaries? Show how the responses to this crisis by the Paris population and the legislators of the National Assembly underlined the divisions created by the Revolution.
3. In August 1791, slaves in France's most valuable colony, Saint-Domingue, began a major revolt. Explain why this uprising was so significant. Why were the French revolutionaries, who had proclaimed in 1789 that all men had a natural right to liberty, so reluctant to abolish slavery?
4. On 10 August 1792, an organized uprising in Paris overthrew the constitutional monarchy established by the National Assembly in 1791. Discuss the reasons for this "second" or "radical" revolution. How was it connected to the war that France had declared against the Austrian Empire in April 1792?

Notes

1. Cited in Esther E. Brown, *The French Revolution and the American Man of Letters* (Columbia, Mo., 1951), 82, 91.
2. Cited in John Hall Stewart, ed., *Documentary Survey of the French Revolution* (New York: Macmillan, 1951), 223.
3. Cited in Beik, ed., *French Revolution,* 201.

CHAPTER 5

The Convention and the Radical Republic, 1792–1794

LEARNING OBJECTIVES

After studying this chapter, you will be able to:

- **Define the characteristics of the Revolution's most radical period, including democracy and the policy of terror.**
- **Explain the reasons for the victory of the radical Jacobins (Montagnards) and the importance of the Committee of Public Safety.**
- **Analyze the features of the period's revolutionary culture and its relationship to the Montagnards' political and social goals.**
- **List the period's consequences for the rights of women and slaves.**

Like the National Assembly, the National Convention that convened in September 1792 made fundamental changes in French life that broke radically with the past. Even more than the National Assembly, its work has been controversial. To some, this assembly laid the groundwork for the basic institutions that make France a democratic society today. Others see the Convention as a violent and destructive regime comparable to the totalitarian dictatorships of the twentieth century. However it is viewed, no historian can deny that the three years of the Convention's session were among the most momentous in all of French history.

The National Convention was born in crisis, and its entire three-year existence was shaped by a series of urgent problems. The deputies elected in September 1792 had to deal with both the Austro-Prussian invasion and the issue of replacing the constitution so laboriously drawn up by the National Assembly. The 749 new deputies were, on the whole, similar to the members of the outgoing Legislative Assembly. In fact, many had sat in one or the other of the earlier assemblies, since there was no repetition of the "self-denying ordinance" of 1791 that had kept deputies from running for reelection. Lawyers and former government officials, overwhelmingly from bourgeois origins, still predominated. Most of the *conventionnels* were young—two-thirds were under forty-five—and strongly committed to the Revolution. To emphasize the universal nature of their principles, the revolutionaries declared several prominent foreign

MORT DE LOUIS XVI, LE 21 JANVIER 1793

Place de la Concorde : on voit à gauche le socle de la statue de Louis XV déboulonnée

(Extrait des *Révolutions de Paris*)

EXECUTION OF LOUIS XVI

Pictures of the execution of the king, such as this one, helped to convey to the population, even those who could not read, the significance of the action taken on 21 January 1793.

supporters of the movement to be French citizens, and two of them, Thomas Paine and Anacharsis Cloots, a radical Prussian nobleman, were even elected as deputies.

The deputies had little in common with the Parisian sans-culottes or the mass of the peasant population. Most deputies still wanted to govern through orderly legal processes, whereas the sans-culottes considered the crisis facing the Revolution too pressing to be resolved through slow-moving legislative debates. For their part, peasants wanted to see concrete benefits from the Revolution, and they were often hostile to the increasingly radical campaign against the Church. The tension between the lower classes and the Convention continued throughout the new assembly's three-year tenure in office and explains much about the policies it adopted.

The Trial of the King

Even before the arrival of news of the victory at Valmy, the Convention had set its political course. In its opening session on 20 September 1792, the deputies immediately voted to proclaim France a republic and thus cut the last institutional link between the Revolution and the Old Regime. But what was to be done with Louis XVI? The debate on his fate split the Convention between the Girondins and the Montagnards, the two factions that had formed during the period of the Legislative Assembly and that now competed to win the votes of the undecided deputies, the "Plain," who held the balance in the new assembly. The Montagnards and Girondins had both participated in the campaign against the king that had begun with the military defeats of June 1792. Even as the pressure to remove Louis

XVI mounted, however, the Girondins had begun to reconsider the idea of provoking popular violence to force him out of office. The September massacres made the Girondins even more wary of the sans-culottes.

The more radical Montagnards now controlled the Jacobin Club. Their most prominent leader was Maximilien Robespierre, known for his speeches on behalf of the less privileged during the National Assembly. In the Convention, his main allies were Danton, who had dominated the government in the critical days between the 10 August insurrection and the convening of the new legislature, and the journalist Marat. Compared with the Girondins, the Montagnards voiced greater concern for the lower classes. Their rhetoric tended to be more moralistic than the Girondins', and their political positions more uncompromising. They favored the abolition of the monarchy and defended the September massacres as a necessary act of self-defense against the Revolution's opponents.

Even though the 1791 constitution had declared the king legally immune to punishment, pressure for action against him was too strong to be resisted. The Montagnards and the sans-culotte leaders contended that no trial was necessary: the king's guilt was obvious, and he should be executed forthwith. A majority of the Convention decided, however, to follow legal procedures and give the king a trial, with the deputies voting on his fate. The legislators thus set the stage for a great public drama that would do much to define the nature of the radical revolution.

Louis was aided by a legal team headed by one of his prerevolutionary ministers, Lamoignon de Malesherbes, who later paid with his life for volunteering for this role. His lawyers argued that the Convention had no legal authority to judge the king, and they reminded the deputies that the king had convoked the Estates-General in 1789 and approved its initial reforms. Determined to maintain his dignity, even in defeat, Louis XVI told the deputies, "In speaking to you, perhaps for the last time, I declare to you that my conscience reproaches me for nothing..."[1] The evidence of his contacts with the émigrés and with the Austrian government, much of it furnished by documents discovered in the *armoire de fer,* a secret safe found in the Tuileries palace after the 10 August uprising, convinced an overwhelming majority of deputies to judge the king guilty of "attempts against liberty and of conspiracy against the general security of the state."[2]

The deputies then had to decide on the king's punishment. The Girondins, seeking some way to avoid the irreparable step of execution, suggested several alternatives. Thomas Paine wanted to banish Louis to the United States. Other Girondin leaders called for a national referendum in which the citizens themselves would determine the king's fate. The Montagnards responded that delaying his punishment would plunge the country into confusion and undermine the war effort. Their most effective orator, the twenty-five-year-old Louis-Antoine Saint-Just, declared that "those who worry about whether it is fair to punish a king will never establish a republic."[3] The final vote was close, with a number of legislators still hoping to find a compromise that would postpone the king's death, but a narrow majority favored immediate execution.

On 21 January 1793, the king was conveyed from his prison to the large public square now known as the Place de la Concorde. The crowd lining the streets was mostly silent. When the king tried to make a final speech from the scaffold, the National Guard commander ordered his drummers to drown him out. The fall of the guillotine's blade underscored the radical turn that the Revolution had taken on 10 August 1792: the Convention had irreversibly ruled out any compromise with the Revolution's opponents.

Mounting Tensions

There was also no compromise in the factional struggle that divided the Convention. The resulting instability became more and more dangerous as the problems facing the Convention became more critical. In the fall of 1792, the French armies had followed up the success at Valmy by invading parts of Belgium and southern Germany. With French support, German supporters of the Revolution established a republican regime in the city of Mainz, the first attempt to copy the French example in other countries. By early 1793, however, France faced new foes. Britain, the Netherlands, and Spain entered the war in February 1793; the British fleet blockaded French ports and threatened France's colonies. By March 1793, the Austrians had regained the initiative in Belgium and the Rhineland, putting an end to the Mainz republic. At the beginning of April, Dumouriez, the defeated French commander in Belgium, tried to lead his troops against the Convention and then went over to the enemy, leaving the main French army in disarray. The fact that he had been friendly with members of the Girondin group offered the Montagnards a new opening to attack their rivals.

The French had hoped that the United States, whose independence France had helped win, would join their struggle against the monarchies of Europe. A French diplomat, Edmond Genet, arrived there in April 1793, planning to license privateers in American ports to prey on British shipping and to organize troops to attack their positions west of the Appalachians. Genet received an enthusiastic welcome from some Americans, but even Thomas Jefferson, who sympathized with the French movement, was determined to keep the country neutral in the fight between Britain and France. In July 1793, the arrival of a wave of refugees fleeing the slave uprising in the French colony of Saint-Domingue alarmed Americans in the slave states. By August, the American government had decided to expel Genet; the two revolutionary republics were rapidly drifting apart.

Danger to the Revolution was also mounting at home. In March, an attempt to draft new troops for the army set off an uprising in rural western France, centered in the department of the Vendée. The peasants who started the insurrection recruited local nobles with military experience to lead them; by June, their "Catholic and Royal Army" had grown to 40,000. The rebellion became a veritable civil war, marked by atrocities on both sides. The Vendeans briefly threatened the port city of Nantes, the capture of which would have allowed them to receive support from England. Although resistance to conscription set off the uprising, the Vendeans had broader grievances against the Revolution. The deeply Catholic rural population in western France rejected the reform of the Church, and many peasants had had to watch as the pro-revolutionary town-dwellers in their region bought up the former Church lands put on sale. The Convention deputies, unwilling to admit that the Revolution's actions might have alienated the rural population, blamed the uprising on priests and nobles. Republican forces used drastic methods to suppress the movement, included mass drownings of prisoners in the Loire river and the burning down of entire villages, together with the massacre of their inhabitants. The Vendée war was the bloodiest episode of the Revolution, claiming perhaps as many as 200,000 lives. It is impossible to justify the excesses committed by the revolutionary forces, but civil wars, especially when they coincide with foreign invasions, as the Vendée rebellion did, frequently set off deadly spirals of violence. Revolutionary leaders in Paris realized that the brutalities committed in the Vendée threatened to discredit them, and such methods were rarely used elsewhere; the deputy on mission Carrier, responsible for many of the mass killings, was recalled after three months.

In addition to the war and the Vendée rebellion, the Convention had to deal with a worsening economic crisis. A poor grain harvest in 1792 sent food prices soaring, and inflation undermined the assignats, the paper currency that the National Assembly had begun to issue in 1789. Wages failed to keep up with the rise in prices, leading to popular protests. To calm the unrest, the Convention passed a law setting maximum prices for wheat and flour and giving the government the right to requisition supplies from reluctant growers. The maximum was a major deviation from the Revolution's original support for free-market principles. Its enactment showed the Convention's growing fear of the popular movement. It also showed the legislators' willingness to meet crises by restricting the individual freedoms guaranteed in the Declaration of the Rights of Man and strengthening the powers of the national government.

The Victory of the Montagnards

In the face of the mounting pressure from the sans-culottes, the split between the Girondins and the Montagnards became more and more bitter. The Girondins supported a new constitutional plan, introduced in February 1793 by Condorcet, one of their leaders, that would have allowed for popular referendums to overturn legislation. The Montagnards condemned the plan as unworkable and as a plot to turn the country against Paris. When there was renewed rioting against high food prices in February and March 1793, the Girondins set a precedent that was later used against them by stripping the Montagnard journalist-deputy Marat of his parliamentary immunity and having him tried by a special court, the Revolutionary Tribunal, for inciting violence. His acquittal sparked sans-culotte demonstrations that showed the Girondins how unpopular they had become among the Paris population.

The political crisis in the Convention had echoes throughout the country, as moderates and radicals struggled for control of local governments. In several big provincial cities, violent local disputes pitted moderate and radical republicans against each other. By the end of May, enemies of the Montagnards controlled such strategic centers as Lyon, Marseille, Bordeaux, and Caen. In concert with the Girondin deputies in Paris, who were supported by a number of the most influential newspapers, these anti-Montagnard groups denounced the excessive influence of Paris on the Convention. It was undemocratic, they asserted, for the Paris sans-culotte activists to be able to impose their political demands, while the views of the provinces were ignored.

To the Montagnard leaders and to the sans-culotte militants in Paris, this challenge cried out for action before it was too late. On 31 May 1793, the radical Paris sections staged a repetition of the 10 August 1792 insurrection: National Guard units, by this time made up mostly of sans-culottes, surrounded the Convention, and two days later the intimidated assembly suspended twenty-nine Girondin deputies. The defeated Girondin leaders fled to the provinces. The Montagnards were left in control of the Convention, which itself was clearly at the mercy of whoever could command the armed sans-culotte battalions.

As a result of the journée of 31 May–2 June 1793, the Montagnards now had unchallenged control of the Convention. On 24 June, the deputies hurriedly endorsed a new constitution to replace the now-defunct document of 1791. The provisions of this Constitution of 1793 were much more democratic than those of its predecessor. It called for a unicameral legislative assembly chosen by universal manhood suffrage, eliminating the distinction between active and passive citizens. Although it continued to safeguard property rights, the 1793 constitution also defined a "right of subsistence," entitling all citizens either to a job or to adequate welfare benefits, and it promised a system of universal free public education. These provisions anticipated modern-day social-welfare legislation in most Western countries. If the government violated the people's rights, the 1793 constitution explicitly recognized their right to rise up against it. The provisions of the Constitution of 1793 were never put into effect, however. The Convention voted to postpone its inauguration until the crisis facing the country had been overcome.

Although the Montagnards now dominated the Convention, they seemed likely to lose much of the rest of the country. France's foreign enemies continued their advances, the Vendée rebels remained a threat, and there was a new danger: a series of revolts against the Jacobin-dominated Convention in some of the major provincial cities. These uprisings, known as the federalist movement, took place in towns whose deputies had been among the purged Girondins and where local governments had been taken over by their supporters, places such as Caen, Bordeaux, Lyon, and Marseille. Unlike the Vendée rebels, the federalists proclaimed their loyalty to the Revolution and the Republic. But they condemned the influence of the radical sans-culotte movement and the centralization of authority in Paris.

Luckily for the Convention, the revolts in different parts of the country remained uncoordinated, and the federalists' essentially negative program failed to rally widespread support, whereas the Convention had the advantage of being the focus of patriotic resistance to the foreign threat. Members of the Convention sent to the provinces as "deputies on mission" with powers to override or replace military commanders and to purge local governments galvanized the war effort against both domestic and foreign enemies while creating a direct link between the population and the government. As the Convention's forces advanced on the federalist strongholds, the republican rebels in Lyon accepted support from avowed royalists. In the Mediterranean port city of Toulon, rebels even welcomed the British fleet. These alliances further discredited the insurrections. The federalist movement, together with Charlotte Corday's assassination of the journalist-deputy Marat on 13 July 1793, added to the Montagnards' sense of being under siege and made them even more reluctant to compromise with opponents. They put down the provincial rebellions with the utmost severity. At Lyon, cannon loaded with chain shot were used to mow down hundreds of captured rebels in a mass execution that was intended to dramatize the Revolution's determination to stamp out its enemies. The Convention even tried to remove the rebel city's name from the map: Lyon was to be renamed "Liberated City."

Terror Becomes the Order of the Day

Although the Montagnard-dominated Convention was able to overcome the federalist revolts during the summer of 1793, its control of the streets of the capital was still not secure. The sans-culotte movement that had helped the Montagnards defeat the Girondins continued to demand ever more radical measures to ensure that the Revolution benefited the common people. Sans-culotte spokesmen advocated direct participatory democracy. They insisted on the primacy of the Paris sections, the forty-eight neighborhood assemblies where any citizen could join the political debates. The sans-culottes' grievances were articulated most forcefully by several agitators and journalists who came to be known as the *enragés*. The best known was the "red priest" Jacques Roux, a former clergyman. He and the other enragé leaders accused the Convention of favoring the wealthy. They demanded price controls, measures against hoarding and speculation in foodstuffs, and severe punishment of the "conspirators" they blamed for the suffering of the poor. (See Document G.)

The enragés' program appealed strongly to the lower classes in Paris and especially to women. Traditionally responsible for buying their families' food, they were especially aware of the increase in bread prices. In May 1793, the most militant women activists formed the Society of Revolutionary Republican Women under the leadership of the actress Claire Lacombe. Although the number of articulate women activists was small, they were often able to draw larger groups into street demonstrations. Women's participation in revolutionary politics reached its peak in the spring and summer of 1793.

DOCUMENT G

The Sans-Culottes and the Enragés

The radical journalist Jacques Hébert, known as the "Père Duchesne," furnished this definition of a sans-culotte:

"A being who always goes on foot, who has no millions, . . . no castle, no valets to serve him, and who lives simply with his wife and children. . . . He is useful, because he knows how to plow a field, to forge, to saw, to file, to roof a building, to make shoes, and to spill out his last drop of blood for the salvation of the Republic." (Cited in William Sewell, *Work and Revolution in France* [Cambridge: Cambridge University Press, 1980] p. 110.)

In the summer of 1793, the former priest Jacques Roux, the leader of the radical group known as the enragés, expressed the dissatisfaction of the poorer members of the Paris population in a speech to the National Convention.

"Delegates of the people, for a long time you have promised to end the calamities the people are suffering from, but what have you done about it? You have just finished writing a constitution that you are going to submit to a vote of the people. But did you include a ban against speculation in it? No! Did you announce punishments for hoarders and monopolists? No! All right: we tell you that you haven't finished the job. . . . Take care, the friends of equality won't be fooled by charlatans who want to contain them through famine, by these vile hoarders whose warehouses are the gathering-places of cheats. . . . What could possibly be the goal of those speculators who take over factories, commerce, and the products of the earth, except to drive the people to despair and force them to throw themselves into the arms of despotism? How long will you allow rich egoists to drink the people's pure blood from gilded cups?...

"No doubt suffering is unavoidable in a great revolution, and we intend to make all the sacrifices necessary to maintain liberty. But the people remembers that it has been betrayed twice by two different assemblies. It is time for the sans-culottes, who have broken the scepter of tyrants, to overthrow every kind of tyranny. Find a quick remedy for our urgent problems."

(From Buchez and Roux, *Histoire parlementaire*, vol. 28, pp. 216–217. Translation by Jeremy D. Popkin.)

The deputies responded to the crisis atmosphere with a series of new measures, such as imposing the death penalty for hoarding grain. On 23 August 1793, the Convention voted the *levée en masse*. For the first time in modern history, the entire population of a country was called upon to rally to its defense, and the entire national economy was, in theory, put under government control. According to the terms of the law, "young men shall go to battle; married men shall forge arms and transport provisions; women shall make tents and clothes, and shall serve in the hospitals...." Even children and the aged were to contribute whatever help they could. State-owned workshops were set up to produce weapons for the army, and the entire population was mobilized to hunt for saltpeter deposits that could be used to make gunpowder. The revolutionaries thus asserted a democratic nation-state's right to conscript all citizens and all resources to meet a national emergency. The limitations the men of 1789 had attempted to impose on governmental power were swept away, and the revolutionary regime established a precedent that would be copied extensively in the wars and revolutions of the twentieth century.

The Convention delegated day-to-day responsibility for running the government to its Committee of Public Safety. This body, first set up in April 1793, had been reconstituted after the defeat of the Girondins. Robespierre, Saint-Just, and several other Montagnard leaders replaced more moderate deputies and gave the Committee's policies a radical direction. Within the Committee, some members handled particular problems: Lazare Carnot directed the armies, Robert Lindet dealt with finances. Others, like Robespierre himself, had a more general role. All Committee members participated in its spirited, often angry debates over major policies. To ensure that its policies were carried out, the Committee tightened its control over the numerous "deputies on mission" or replaced them with its own agents.

The levée en masse and the establishment of the "great" Committee were major steps toward the consolidation of a revolutionary dictatorship. The sans-culotte leaders remained unsatisfied, however. On 5 September 1793, an armed crowd once again surrounded the Convention, demanding that it make "terror the order of the day." To calm the crowd, the deputies added two prominent radicals, Collot d'Herbois and Billaud-Varennes, to the Committee of Public Safety. In the weeks that followed, the Convention passed a further series of laws to strengthen government powers and to show its revolutionary zeal. These new laws ensured that the government of France would remain "revolutionary until the peace," as a decree passed on 10 October 1793 put it. For the next ten months, France lived under a full-fledged revolutionary dictatorship, in which almost all individual rights were suspended.

On 29 September, the Convention voted a general maximum, extending the price controls earlier imposed on grain to a long list of products classified as "necessities" and setting workers' wages at a level meant to raise living standards above what they had been in 1790. "Revolutionary armies" of militant sans-culottes were sent to the countryside to force reluctant farmers to turn over requisitioned grain. The government also imposed censorship to silence political opposition. The "law of suspects," passed on 17 September, set up surveillance committees throughout the country. They were ordered to list all people "who, by their conduct, associations, talk, or writings have shown themselves…enemies of liberty." "Suspects" could be jailed indefinitely. The Revolutionary Tribunal tried and convicted a number of prominent political figures: the Queen, the Girondin leaders, and such symbols of the liberal revolution of 1789 as Barnave and Bailly, the mayor of Paris who had put down the Champ de Mars demonstration in July 1791. Their executions dramatized the revolutionary government's rejection of both the monarchy and the earlier, more moderate phases of the Revolution itself. Suspicious of traitors, the revolutionaries also turned against even those foreigners who supported their cause. Paine and Cloots, elected to the Convention in 1792, were deprived of their seats and arrested in December 1793, and a law of April 1794 barred all foreigners from Paris and strategic areas of the country.

The Dictatorship of the Committee of Public Safety

The revolutionary dictatorship set up in the fall of 1793 fulfilled many of the sans-culotte movement's demands. But it did so by creating a powerful centralized government that increasingly made itself independent of the Paris popular movement. By giving the Committee of Public Safety the authority to nominate members of all its other committees and appoint deputies on mission, the Convention made it the real center of the government. The Convention had to vote to renew the Committee's membership and its powers every thirty days. In the crisis atmosphere that prevailed until the summer of 1794, however, there was little chance of the deputies' deciding to revoke the Committee's authority. The Committee gave orders to the ministers and the commanding generals of the French armies. It worked closely with the Committee of General Security, which oversaw the police. That committee's *mouchards*, or spies, listened to conversations in the streets and cabarets, and kept the government informed about public opinion.

A law passed on 4 December 1793 specified that the Convention's decrees took precedence over all local measures and gave the central government authority to remove and replace local administrators, reversing the movement toward decentralization that had characterized the liberal stage of the Revolution. This centralized power was enhanced by the tremendous growth in the government's bureaucracy: hundreds of new clerks were hired to see that the new laws were carried out. In the provinces, local Jacobin militants threw themselves into implementing national policies. Urged on by deputies sent from Paris, they denounced violators of the maximum, identified suspects, helped recruit soldiers, and organized care for the wounded. This largely improvised system, dependent on enthusiastic amateurs, nevertheless permitted the Montagnards to govern the country more effectively than any of the earlier revolutionary regimes.

Both contemporaries and historians have recognized Maximilien Robespierre as the leading figure among the Committee of Public Safety's members. Although he came from a modest background and often spoke of his love for the common people, Robespierre had little in common with them. He was an educated intellectual especially influenced by Rousseau's writings. A man with few friends, Robespierre was nevertheless a skillful politician. His carefully thought-out speeches helped maintain support for the government in the Convention and the Jacobin Club. His reputation for disinterested devotion to the public good gave him the nickname "the Incorruptible." In the end, Robespierre would be brought down by his obsession with the vision of an ideal republic and his indifference to the human cost of installing it, but historians who see him as nothing more than a ruthless fanatic overlook his equally real commitment to the principles of democracy, the basis of his popular support.

Robespierre was better known than his colleagues on the Committee of Public Safety because he was called on most often to justify its actions and the system of revolutionary government. His speech of 25 December 1793 argued that a temporary dictatorship was the only way to achieve the constitutional freedoms that had been the original object of the Revolution. "Revolution is the war waged by liberty against its enemies; a constitution is that which crowns the edifice of freedom once victory has been won and the nation is at peace," he said. Until the "enemies of the people" who opposed the movement had been definitively defeated, Robespierre argued, the government had to have virtually unlimited powers. "Those who call them arbitrary or tyrannical," he thundered, "are foolish or perverse sophists who seek to reconcile white with black and black with white: They prescribe the same system for peace and war, for health and sickness...."[4] (See Document H.)

This doctrine clearly reflected the circumstances of 1793, in which the men of the Convention had to combat armed enemies on all sides and to take extraordinary measures to keep the population fed. But the idea of using the power of an unfettered government to remake the French people tempted the Montagnard leaders. In a manuscript he left unpublished, Robespierre's young colleague Saint-Just sketched an austere modern-day Sparta, in which children would be taken from their parents at the age of seven and raised in state schools, so that their only loyalty would be to the nation. Robespierre talked of a Republic of Virtue, from which private selfishness would be banished. "All has changed in the physical order; all must change in the moral and political order. One half of the world revolution is already achieved, the other half has yet to be accomplished...," he wrote, suggesting an almost limitless program.[5]

Revolutionary Culture

The dream of creating a moralized revolutionary utopia was embodied in efforts to create a new revolutionary culture. On 5 October 1793, the Convention replaced the Christian calendar with a new revolutionary one, meant to show that the Revolution had begun a new era in human history. Years were to be counted from the establishment of the French Republic on 22 September 1792, so that 1793–1794 became the

Year II. The year was divided into twelve months, each given a poetic name based on its weather—*nivôse* was the month of snow, *floréal* the month when flowers bloomed—and each month was divided into three ten-day weeks, or *décades*.

The new calendar was part of a program of rationalization that included the introduction of the metric system on 1 August 1793, a reform that lasted, and the division of the day into ten hundred-minute hours, which did not. But it was also related to the de-Christianization campaign that reached its height in late 1793. Whereas the National Assembly had intended to reform the Church, the de-Christianizers aimed to abolish it altogether. The movement was initiated by revolutionary militants in provincial areas where anticlerical attitudes were already strong at the end of the Old Regime. They accused Catholic priests of "having kept us stupid, kept our souls enchained by absurd mysteries, play-acting and useless ceremonies."[6] Activists intimidated priests and nuns into renouncing their vows and marrying. They destroyed religious statuary and confiscated church buildings for granaries and other secular purposes.

DOCUMENT H

Robespierre on the Terror, 1793

In his speech on revolutionary government, Robespierre defended extraordinary measures as necessary to create conditions in which true liberty could flourish.

"The theory of revolutionary government is as new as the Revolution that created it. It is as pointless to seek its origins in the books of the political theorists, who failed to foresee this revolution, as in the laws of the tyrants, who are happy enough to abuse their exercise of authority without seeking out its legal justification.... It behooves us to explain it to all in order that we may rally good citizens, at least, in support of the principles governing the public interest."

"It is the function of government to guide the moral and physical energies of the nation toward the purposes for which it was established."

"The object of constitutional government is to preserve the Republic; the object of revolutionary government is to establish it."

"Revolution is the war waged by liberty against its enemies; a constitution is that which crowns the edifice of freedom once victory has been won and the nation is at peace."

"The revolutionary government has to summon extraordinary activity to its aid precisely because it is at war. It is subjected to less binding and less uniform regulations, because the circumstances in which it finds itself are tempestuous and shifting, above all because it is compelled to deploy, swiftly and incessantly, new resources to meet new and pressing dangers."

The principal concern of constitutional government is civil liberty; that of revolutionary government, public liberty. Under a constitutional government little more is required than to protect the individual against abuses by the state, whereas revolutionary government is obliged to defend the state itself against the factions that assail it from every quarter.

"To good citizens revolutionary government owes the full protection of the state; to the enemies of the people it owes only death."

(From George Rudé, ed., *Robespierre* [Upper Saddle River, N.J.: Prentice Hall, 1967] pp. 58–59. Reprinted by permission of the publisher.)

In November 1793, the de-Christianizers turned Paris's Notre Dame Cathedral into a Temple of Reason and staged a ceremony in honor of a Goddess of Liberty, impersonated by an actress from the Opera. Robespierre and the leaders of the Convention kept their distance from the de-Christianization campaign and eventually reined it in: they feared its potential for further inflaming religious conflict. To much of the French population, de-Christianization proved what devout Catholics had claimed at the time of the earlier Church reforms: the Revolution was the enemy of religion. The split between Catholics and ardent republicans was to remain one of the main divisions in French life for well over a century.

The revolutionaries also undertook to root out dialect languages and regional cultures, which they saw as threats to national unity. If the Breton peasants resisted the Revolution, one deputy asserted, it was because "they speak a language as different from ours as German or English."[7] Revolutionary militants sought to use language to propagate the new values of the revolutionary regime. They encouraged their fellow citizens to address each other with the familiar *tu* rather than the more formal *vous* that had traditionally been used to show respect for social superiors. Instead of calling each other *Monsieur*, men addressed each other as *citoyen* ("citizen"). In the colonies, officials tried to abolish the use of terms that differentiated between whites and the free people of color who had been granted equal status in 1792. By promoting a national language and doing away with words that recalled the difference between classes, supporters of the Revolution hoped to create a national community of equal citizens.

The revolutionaries of the Year II used theater, art, and other media to propagate new symbols and new values. On public buildings and government agencies' letterheads, slogans like "Liberty, Equality, Fraternity, or Death" and icons like an all-seeing eye, a reminder of the vigilance that every patriot was expected to maintain, replaced the symbols of Catholicism and the monarchy. Revolutionary playing cards featured effigies of Liberty or portraits of the philosophes in place of kings and queens. Jacques-Louis David, the country's most prominent artist, put his talents to use for the revolutionary cause. His posthumous portrait of the assassinated Montagnard journalist Marat, the one real masterpiece of painting from the revolutionary decade, used the techniques normally employed to depict the crucified Christ to glorify the memory of an actual historical figure. David also designed the decorations and costumes for the elaborate public festivals, such as the Festival of the Supreme Being, that were a major part of the Montagnards' cultural campaign. This revolutionary cultural propaganda strengthened the consciousness of a break with the past at the level of everyday life, but its enforced nature created much resentment against the new regime.

The Radical Revolution and the Social Order

Along with their program of cultural transformation, the Montagnards also enacted a number of measures meant to favor the lower classes. In the countryside, peasants had acted to defend their interests without waiting for approval from the Convention. They refused to make the compensation payments to their landlords that the decrees of 4 August 1789 had called for, and they defended communal rights that the legislators had tried to abolish. Shaken by the peasant revolt in the Vendée and rural uprisings in parts of southern France, the deputies passed several laws aimed at satisfying peasant demands. The redemption payments for feudal dues were abolished, and the deputies passed a law to promote the division of village common lands, meant to give even the poorest peasants a chance to acquire some property. The Convention also ordered that Church and émigré lands put up for auction be divided into smaller lots so that peasant bidders would have a better chance of purchasing them. In February 1794, the Convention, at Saint-Just's urging, passed its most radical social legislation, the so-called ventôse decrees, which called for the confiscated estates of counterrevolutionaries to be divided up and distributed free to indigent patriots. Twentieth-century Marxist historians interpreted the ventôse decrees as a sign that the revolutionary government was ready to question the sanctity of private property. In practice, however, this radical proposal was never really implemented.

Although women were prominent in the radical movements that had brought the Montagnards to power in 1793, the Convention now began to treat them as a source of disorder. In November 1793, it banned all public political activity by women and closed down the most important of the women's political clubs, the Society of Revolutionary Republican Women, for promoting street agitation. At the Paris Commune, the sans-culotte leader Chaumette claimed that "it is contrary to all the laws of nature for a woman to want to make herself a man" by taking on public responsibilities. Women were to confine themselves to the home, where they could serve the nation by raising their children as patriots.[8] Accused of counterrevolutionary tendencies, several women activists, including Olympe de Gouges, were guillotined.

Excluded from the revolutionary movement, some women turned against it. Female participation in bread riots had served to radicalize the Revolution in 1789, but by 1794 such protests often expressed counterrevolutionary sentiments. Women were prominent in many protests against the Civil Constitution of the Clergy. Many historians have concluded that it was during the revolutionary period that the division between a male population attracted to liberal and rationalist ideas and a female population loyal to traditional religious beliefs, which was to characterize France throughout the nineteenth century, first emerged.

Although the Montagnard Convention excluded women from the public sphere, it took an important symbolic step by becoming the first European government to abolish slavery and grant full political rights to blacks. The fighting that had continued in the key French colony of Saint-Domingue since the slave revolt of August 1791 prompted this step. The Legislative Assembly had dispatched commissioners and troops to the island in September 1792. Fearing resistance from the white colonists, the republican commissioners initially promised to maintain slavery. Their insistence on enforcing French laws granting equal rights to free people of color alienated most of the white population, however, many of whom were prepared to accept British and Spanish intervention. When white opponents of the commissioners tried to capture the island's main city, Cap Français, in June 1793, the commissioners offered freedom to black slaves who joined their forces. In the months that followed, this was extended to a general policy of emancipation of the colony's entire slave population. Three deputies to the Convention—a white man, a black man, and a man of mixed race—were chosen to bring news of these developments to France. Their arrival in February 1794 spurred the Convention to decree the abolition of slavery in all the French colonies. France became the first country to

DOCUMENT I

Gender and Conformity during the Terror

In mid-February 1794, a young mother brought her six-year-old daughter to a session of Paris's municipal assembly, the Commune, where the little girl recited some patriotic verses. The official newspaper of the Jacobin movement, the *Journal de la Montagne*, reported the response of Pierre Chaumette, one of the Commune's officials, which is revealing about attitudes toward women and how revolutionary culture turned into a system of forced conformism:

"Chaumette said that one couldn't blame the mother, who no doubt thought she was doing a good thing in getting her daughter to learn these verses, but he told her... that such things should not make up the earliest education of a little girl. 'Teach her to knit stockings,' he said, 'and when she has made a pair of them, bring her back, and we'll vote her civic honors.' 'I can't teach her to knit stockings,' the mother replied. 'I only know how to sew.' 'In that case, teach her to sew!' And that concluded this confrontation over republican behavior, which should put useful things ahead of decorative ones."

(From *Journal de la Montagne*, 23 plu. II. Translation by Jeremy D. Popkin.)

take such action, and the deputy J.-B. Belley, a former slave, became the first black man to sit in a European legislature. The effect of the Convention's action remained dependent on the outcome of the war, however: at the moment when it was passed, the British had occupied France's two other Caribbean colonies, Guadeloupe and Martinique, as well as a portion of Saint-Domingue.

The Great Terror and Thermidor

Obsessed with maintaining national unity, the Montagnard leaders engaged in a constantly intensifying hunt for hidden conspirators whose activities they blamed for the Revolution's continuing difficulties. Increasingly, those who fell under suspicion were the Revolution's own supporters, creating what historian Marisa Linton has called a "politicians' terror." Those who held leading positions in the revolutionary movement were increasingly exposed to mortal danger themselves. Already in 1793, the arrested Girondin deputy Vergniaud had commented prophetically that "the Revolution, like Saturn, is devouring its children." Tension and fear among the political leaders reached a peak with two spectacular show trials in March and April 1794, meant to eliminate "factions" whose leaders challenged the authority of the Committee of Public Safety.

First, the Committee of Public Safety arrested the most prominent spokesmen of the Paris sans-culotte movement. The journalist Jacques Hébert, author of the *Père Duchêne*, the pamphlet-journal that had become the symbol of radical patriotism, and several of his supporters were tried and executed on trumped-up charges. Their execution was intended to forestall any further sans-culotte agitation against the Committee's policies. Already in the previous fall, the Convention had limited the Paris sections to two public meetings a week, and by voting to pay those who attended section meetings, it had deprived those assemblies of their spontaneous character. An extensive police network made sure that there would be no repetitions of the bread riots and protests that had been so frequent in 1792 and 1793.

Having brought the sans-culotte movement under control, the Committee then turned against the "Indulgents," a group of Convention deputies who had raised their voices against the extension of the Terror and who seemed to have support among the middle classes. Whereas Hébert and his followers had been "ultras" who wanted to push the Revolution too far, Robespierre charged, these men—particularly the famed orator Danton and the journalist Camille Desmoulins, who had criticized the Committee in his paper, the *Vieux Cordelier*—were "citras" who wanted to stop the Revolution before it had gone far enough. In powerful speeches before the Revolutionary Tribunal, Danton threatened to turn the tables on the Committee and show the baselessness of the charges against him. The Convention hurriedly passed a decree changing the trial procedures to silence him. The Danton group's execution on 5 April 1794 showed that any revolutionary politician, no matter how prominent, could fall victim to the Terror.

Rather than reassuring the Committee, the executions of the Hébertists and Dantonists merely accelerated the Terror's pace. The atmosphere of enforced conformism and the evident lack of genuine enthusiasm that the Terror itself had engendered made the movement's leaders even more fearful. Saint-Just complained that "the Revolution has become frozen" and called for ever more drastic measures against hidden counterrevolutionaries. On 8 June 1794, Robespierre presided over an elaborately staged Festival of the Supreme Being, designed by the artist Jacques-Louis David and meant to demonstrate the nation's spiritual unity and adherence to revolutionary principles. Two days later, Robespierre forced through the Convention a law that stripped suspects sent before the Revolutionary Tribunal of all rights to defend themselves. Convention deputies no longer enjoyed any special immunity from arrest. This "law of 22 prairial" unleashed the so-called Great Terror of the summer of 1794. The pace of executions, which had slowed after the defeat of the federalist revolts, accelerated again. In six weeks, the guillotine decapitated over 1,300 victims in Paris alone; over all, revolutionary tribunals condemned some 17,000 people to death in 1793 and 1794. Altogether, the number of violent deaths during the Terror period probably added up to something between 250,000 and 300,000; the majority of the victims died in the Vendée revolt.

How a revolutionary movement begun in the name of individual liberty could have culminated in so much bloodshed, and how Robespierre, an eloquent advocate of human rights, could have become the Terror's main proponent are questions that continue to be debated after more than two hundred years. Critics of the Revolution, from Edmund Burke to modern historians such as François Furet, have seen the Terror as an outgrowth of the movement's utopian and unrealistic aspirations. Unable to admit that their goal of a perfectly just society was unattainable, Robespierre and his followers blamed all those who refused to accept their leadership; incapable of admitting that differences of opinion could be legitimate, they classified all opponents as enemies and felt justified in condemning them to death. Robespierre's personality—his tendency to think in abstractions, his absolute faith in his own righteousness, and his suspicion of others' motives—made him especially prone to resort to punitive measures, regardless of their human cost.

Supporters of the Revolution at the time and a long line of subsequent historians, including both liberals and Marxists, have countered this analysis by blaming the

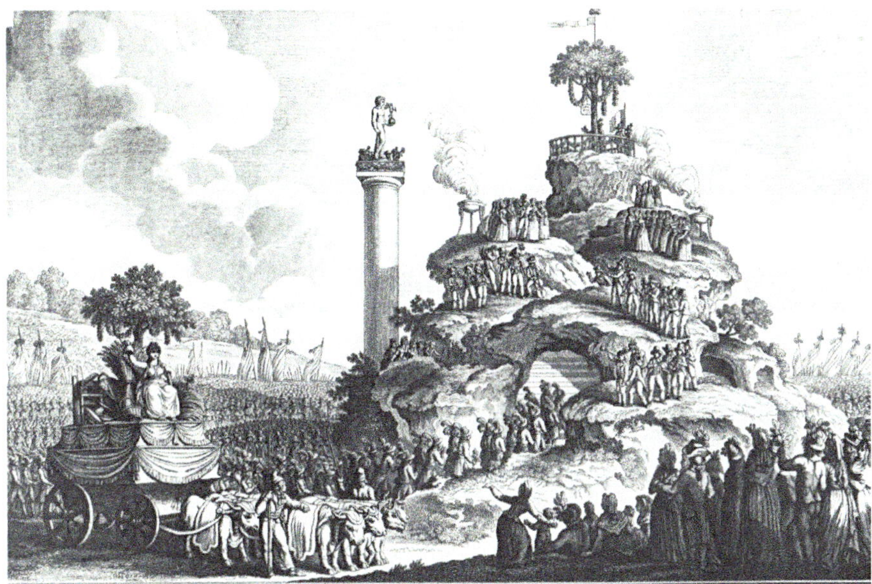

FESTIVAL OF THE SUPREME BEING

On 8 June 1794, Robespierre presided over an elaborate "Festival of the Supreme Being," staged by Jacques-Louis David, the leading revolutionary artist. An artificial mountain, topped by a liberty tree, was constructed on the Champ de Mars to represent the triumph of the Montagnards in the Convention; a giant statue of Hercules on a pillar stood for the French people. Other symbols conveyed the message that the Revolution had restored French society to harmony with nature. Two days after this celebration of harmony, the Convention passed the drastic law of 22 prairial II, allowing the excesses of the Great Terror.

Terror primarily on the difficult circumstances that the revolutionaries had to face. From the outset, the Revolution's enemies were themselves ready to resort to force to oppose the movement. Furthermore, the revolutionary leadership had to take forceful measures to prevent even bloodier outbreaks of popular violence; the legalized Terror was an effort to forestall uncontrolled massacres such as those of September 1792. Historians who see the Terror as explicable in these terms recognize Robespierre's central role in its dangerous expansion in 1794 but they also cite signs that he was looking for a way to bring the uncontrolled killing to an end, perhaps by using the Law of Suspects against the most violent advocates of the guillotine. If so, however, he was unable to achieve his purpose before he himself fell victim to the deadly political rules he had helped establish.

The Revolution Victorious

The Great Terror peaked just as the real dangers to the republican government's security were fading. Even before the last of the federalist uprisings in the south had been defeated, the French armies on the frontiers, their numbers swollen by the levée en masse, had regained the initiative against the Austrians and their allies. To replace the many noble commanders who had fled abroad, the Convention promoted patriotic officers from the lower ranks who had demonstrated their abilities, creating a group of young, daring generals devoted to the republican cause. The Committee of Public Safety took charge of overall strategy. From Paris, Carnot sent orders to the field armies and ruthlessly weeded out the timid and incompetent, executing defeated commanders and even some generals who won battles but failed to pursue the beaten enemy with sufficient vigor. Deputies on mission made sure the Committee's orders were carried out. The troops were formed into new units under a policy known as the *amalgame*, in which the separate units of veteran soldiers from the old royal army and draftees and volunteers of the new citizen force were melded together. The new mixed units thus combined experience and patriotic enthusiasm.

By late 1793, the French armies had learned to make good use of the modernized, mobile artillery developed at the end of the Old Regime to support the spirit and courage of their citizen soldiers. The hastily recruited soldiers could not execute the elaborate maneuvers customary in eighteenth-century warfare, but they proved successful when they were deployed in loose formations or assembled into large columns for charging enemy lines. As the army won battles, the soldiers came to identify more strongly with the cause they fought for. "Ah! How the first laurels thrill any generous and patriotic heart! I don't think that the joys of love can make a livelier impression," one volunteer later wrote.[9] In September 1793, the French victory at Hondschoote forced the English to lift the siege of Dunkirk. The following month, a victory at Wattignies drove the Austrians back into Belgium. The Spanish thrust into Roussillon was beaten off, and in December, a young artillery officer then known as Napoleone Buonaparte distinguished himself by ousting the English from Toulon. French forces were less successful at sea, but by June 1794, the navy, virtually immobilized by mutinies a year earlier, was strong enough to risk a major engagement with the British fleet. Although the French suffered heavy losses in what the British labeled "The Glorious First of June," the battle enabled a convoy of merchant ships bringing much-needed supplies from the United States to slip through the British blockade. The Convention hailed this achievement as a French victory. At the battle of Fleurus on 26 June 1794, the French armies in the north decisively defeated the Austrians, who withdrew from Belgium. The danger of foreign invasion could no longer be used to justify the policy of terror.

Thermidor

As the crisis atmosphere of 1793 faded, a number of deputies in the Convention and even some members of the Committee of Public Safety began to turn against Robespierre's terror policy. Some were cautious moderates who had hesitated to speak out when the fate of the Revolution seemed in suspense, but the most active were former terrorists or friends of the Dantonists who feared that Robespierre planned to have them arrested. When Robespierre gave a speech on 8 thermidor (the eleventh month of the revolutionary calendar) denouncing a plot that he said was directed against him, these deputies decided they had to act. On the next day, 9 thermidor (27 July 1794), their leaders took the floor in the Convention to accuse Robespierre of plotting to make himself dictator. The Convention shouted Robespierre down when he tried to reply. The deputies then voted overwhelmingly for the arrest of Robespierre and several of his supporters. Robespierre and his fellow arrestees briefly escaped from their captors and rallied some supporters at the Hôtel-de-Ville, the seat of Paris's city government, where they appealed to the Paris sections to back them. But the mass of the Paris sans-culottes, alienated from the Montagnards by the execution of the Hébertists and the repression of the popular movement, supported the Convention. Early the next day, the Convention's troops captured the escaped prisoners and hustled Robespierre, Saint-Just, and several dozen of their supporters to the guillotine. Once again, the mechanism of the Revolution had turned against those who had set it in motion. But 9 thermidor marked a turning point: instead of intensifying the revolutionary process, the victors, no longer pushed along by organized popular protest, began to dismantle the machinery of the Revolution.

Critical Thinking Questions

1. The overthrow of the monarchy on 10 August 1792 and the election of the National Convention set the stage for the most radical and violent period of the French Revolution. Analyze how this phase of the Revolution differed from the liberal period of 1789–1792.
2. In the course of 1793, the most radical Jacobin revolutionaries created a regime that came to be known as the Reign of Terror. Describe the major features of this form of revolutionary government. Why did the revolutionary leaders think that they needed to establish a form of dictatorship?
3. The radical period of the Revolution had important consequences for the rights of women and those of the slaves in France's colonies. Explain how these two groups were affected by the laws passed during this period. What does the radical revolutionaries' treatment of women and blacks show about their conception of natural rights?
4. During the Reign of Terror, the radical revolutionaries attempted to transform France's culture and "regenerate" its citizens. Describe some of the major changes they attempted to introduce during this period. How were they supposed to reflect the principles of liberty and equality?

Notes

1. Cited in David Jordan, *The King's Trial* (Berkeley: University of California Press, 1979), 136.
2. Ibid., 172.
3. Saint-Just, *Oeuvres choisies* (Paris: Gallimard, 1968), 76.
4. Cited in George Rudé, ed., *Robespierre* (Upper Saddle River, N.J.: Prentice Hall, 1967), 59.
5. Ibid., 69.
6. Cited in Louis Trénard, *Lyon de l'Encyclopédie au préromantisme* (Paris: Presses Universitaires de France, 1958), 365.
7. Cited in Serge Bianchi, *La révolution culturelle de l'an II* (Paris: Aubier, 1982), 197.
8. Cited in Darline Gay Levy and Harriet B. Applewhite, "Women and Militant Citizenship in Revolutionary Paris," in Sara Melzer and Leslie Rabine, eds., *Rebel Daughters: Women and the French Revolution* (New York: Oxford University Press, 1992), 97.
9. Jean François Noel, *L'Ombre et la lumière: Mémoires d'un bourgeois de Dombes.* (Translated by Jeremy D. Popkin.)

CHAPTER 6

The Return to Order, 1794–1799

LEARNING OBJECTIVES

After studying this chapter, you will be able to:

- **Explain the political and social consequences of the overthrow of Robespierre and the "thermidorian reaction."**
- **Describe the consequences of republican France's military expansion from 1794 to 1799.**
- **Analyze the reasons for the Directory regime's inability to win broad public support.**

The "Bourgeois Republic" and the Search for Order

In just five years, from 1789 to 1794, the Revolution had reshaped French society. The revolutionaries had eliminated corporate privileges and given equal rights to all male citizens. They had abolished the monarchy, strengthened the position of the property-owning bourgeoisie and of peasant landholders, redefined the gender division between men and women, and made France the first European country to end slavery in its colonies. They had established a secular society, and they had created a formidable military machine. By doing all this so rapidly, however, the Revolution had shattered the equilibrium of French society. With the fall of Robespierre, the forces of resistance to continual change came to the surface. The dominant theme of the years from 1794 to 1799 was a search for order and political stability, rather than an effort to accomplish further reforms.

The overthrow of Robespierre on 9 thermidor did not immediately result in a change of political institutions. The "thermidorians," as the deputies of the Convention who survived Robespierre came to be known, continued to govern the country for another fifteen months. In October 1795, a new constitution drafted by the Convention went into effect. The new government consisted of a bicameral legislature and a five-man executive committee known as the Directory. The political leaders of the Directory regime, which governed France until 1799, were mostly former Convention deputies, and the policies they followed largely continued those adopted after thermidor, so historians usually treat the period from 1794 to 1799 as a unit.

The thermidorian and Directory governments both claimed to be consolidating the essential achievements of the Revolution, while avoiding the excesses committed during the Reign of Terror. Liberty and equality were still official slogans, the government remained republican in form, and the revolutionary calendar, which glorified the Convention's proclamation of the Republic in September 1792, remained in use. The postthermidorian Republic carried on the war begun in 1792, kept up the struggle against the Catholic Church, and maintained the abolition of slavery in the colonies. The biggest difference in policy between this period and the one that preceded it was in the relationship between the government and the lower classes. Sobered by what they saw as the consequences of unlimited democracy, the thermidorians openly worked to establish a political regime dominated by the wealthy and educated. Only in this way, they believed, could social order be reconciled with a republican form of government.

The Thermidorian Reaction

Initially it was not clear whether the Convention deputies who had overthrown Robespierre also meant to eliminate his methods of government. Many of the leading thermidorian conspirators, such as Fouché, one of the most prominent activists in the de-Christianization movement of 1793, and the deputy Tallien, who had publicly justified the September massacres and directed the repression of the federalist revolt in Bordeaux, had been active in the Terror. But thermidor unleashed a reaction against the Terror and the radical Revolution that soon escaped the plotters' control. For the next five years, the question of how to repudiate the worst excesses committed in 1793–1794 without endangering the Revolution as a whole and all of those who had participated in the revolutionary government dominated French life.

The thermidorian plotters quickly found themselves under pressure to dismantle the dictatorial apparatus of the Terror. The Committee of Public Safety's powers were curtailed and thousands of prisoners arrested under the Law of Suspects were released from prison. Several of the most prominent architects of the Terror, including Carrier, who had overseen the massacres of rebels in Brittany, and Fouquier-Tinville, the prosecutor of the Revolutionary Tribunal, were tried and executed, despite their protests that they had simply carried out policies approved by the Convention as a whole. In November 1794, the Convention ordered the closing of the Paris Jacobin Club. In Paris, bands of elegantly dressed middle-class youths, the *jeunesse dorée* or "gilded youth," harassed former sans-culotte activists and destroyed symbols of the radical Revolution, such as the busts of Marat that had been placed in public buildings after his assassination. In the provinces, similar groups were even more violent; a "white terror" took the place of the "red terror" of 1794 as former Jacobin militants were killed in Lyon, Marseille, and other areas where counterrevolutionary sentiment was strong.

The Defeat of the Sans-Culottes

The "thermidorian reaction" also turned against the social and economic policies adopted in 1793. The Convention dismantled the maximum system and left prices free to find their own levels. Without the threat of the guillotine to sustain it, the assignat rapidly lost all value. This runaway inflation benefited peasants with grain reserves and middle-class speculators but it was devastating to the urban poor, whose wages lagged far behind the skyrocketing price of bread. An exceptionally harsh winter added to their misery.

The Paris sans-culottes reacted to their situation by staging two massive protest demonstrations, the journées of 12–13 germinal III (1–2 April 1795) and 1–4 prairial III (20–23 May 1795). On both occasions, large crowds of men and women from the working-class faubourgs on the edge of the city surrounded the thermidorian Convention's meeting hall. They demanded "bread and the Constitution of 1793," the democratic constitution approved by the Montagnard Convention but never put into effect. The prairial insurrection proved to be the last major episode of violent popular activism during the revolutionary period, and also the last occasion on which women played a leading role in a public demonstration. The angry crowd invaded the Convention and massacred one of the deputies. Under this pressure, a handful of former Montagnard deputies urged their colleagues to take action to satisfy the sans-culottes' demands. The majority of the deputies remained silent, however, and outside the Convention, troops and National Guards from the middle-class districts, assisted by members of the jeunesse dorée, eventually drove the demonstrators back. In the repression that followed, several crowd leaders were executed; sans-culotte activists were forced to give up the weapons they had used in protest marches and were deprived of their political rights. Women were forbidden to assemble in groups of more than five. Six Montagnard deputies who had sided with the demonstrators were tried and sentenced to death. Four of them succeeded in committing suicide before they could be guillotined, winning fame as the "martyrs of prairial." These measures eliminated both the organized popular movement in Paris and the last deputies willing to identify themselves with its demands in the Convention.

The defeat of the popular movement accelerated the reaction against everything associated with the radical phase of the Revolution While the poor continued to struggle to afford bread, the wealthy crowded cafés, restaurants, and theaters where they applauded plays that denounced the horrors of Robespierre's reign and presented the sans-culottes as bloodthirsty monsters. In the streets, the honorific term "Monsieur" ousted the revolutionary "Citizen" as the preferred form of address, and the polite form "vous" regained its ascendancy. Objects of sympathy during the early revolutionary years, the poor were now seen as violent and dangerous, needing to be disciplined by the rigorous workings of economic laws. The thermidorian reaction also affected attitudes toward women and the family. Much of the public now blamed the egalitarian divorce law of 1792 for putting individual interests above those of the family unit, and a 1793 law granting illegitimate children the same inheritance rights as legitimate heirs was repealed.

Counterrevolution and the Constitution of 1795

The prairial uprising convinced the thermidorians of the need for a new constitution to replace the radical plan enacted in 1793 whose application the rioters had been demanding. The discrediting of revolutionary radicalism raised the hopes of counterrevolutionaries, both those inside France and the émigrés abroad. In Paris, even some Convention deputies toyed with the idea of proclaiming Louis XVI's young son as king and setting up a regency council chosen among themselves to govern the country until he reached adulthood. The boy's death, announced on 8 June 1795, scuttled this project, however. Louis XVI's brother, the Comte de Provence, who had fled the country in 1789, proclaimed himself the rightful heir to the throne, calling himself Louis XVIII. From his Italian refuge, he issued the Declaration of Verona, announcing that he intended to restore the privileges of the nobility and the Church and to punish all those who had taken part in the Revolution since its inception. His intransigent position ruled out any possible compromise with the thermidorian deputies.

In western France, the fall of Robespierre allowed the chouan guerrilla forces that had become active during the Vendée rebellion to reorganize themselves. In the spring of 1795, their leaders established contact with the British government and French royalist émigrés across the Channel. The British promised to land an émigré army if the rebels could seize a port on the French coast. Misunderstandings between the French monarchists and their country's traditional enemy crippled this alliance from the start. The British did transport 4,500 French émigrés to the Quiberon peninsula in Brittany at the end of June 1795, but promised reinforcements never arrived. Republican forces under General Hoche quickly surrounded the royalists and forced them to surrender. Under a law requiring the execution of émigrés captured bearing arms, 748 royalist officers were immediately put to death. The Quiberon disaster devastated the émigrés, some of whom accused the British of plotting to kill them off, and weakened the chouan resistance. By mid-1796, Hoche's forces had pacified Brittany and the Vendée.

While the royalist insurrection in the west was being crushed, the thermidorian Convention completed the new Constitution of 1795 (also known as the Constitution of the Year III, according to the republican calendar). Its main aim was to prevent the rise of another dictatorial government. To do this, the thermidorians believed they needed to exclude the common people from politics. The new constitution limited the right to vote and to hold office to the wealthiest taxpayers: only about 30,000 met the requirements to serve in the departmental electoral colleges, where deputies were to be chosen. All references to social rights were eliminated from the constitution, and the deputies added a "declaration of duties" designed to remind the poor of their obligation to respect the rights of property and the authority of the law. (See Document J.)

The administrative system remained highly centralized, but the powers of the central government were carefully divided. The deputies took to heart Sieyès's warning that the Terror had turned the French government into a "Re-Total," invading all aspects of life, rather than a "Re-Public," limited only to those matters that were truly of general concern. To prevent the creation of an all-encompassing central power, executive power was to be shared by the five members of the Directory. Their power was held in check by a two-house legislature, made up of a Council of 500 and a smaller Council of Elders, limited to deputies over forty years of age.

The announcement of a popular referendum to approve the new constitution inspired one more counterrevolutionary assault. In Paris, the sectional assemblies, purged of sans-culotte activists, had been taken over by the most reactionary thermidorians, such as the leaders of the jeunesse dorée. The Convention gave this movement a target by passing a decree requiring voters to choose two-thirds of the deputies for the new Councils from the outgoing members of the Convention. The Convention's intention was to prevent any widespread purge of republicans—exactly what the Paris activists were determined to accomplish. When the Convention refused to count most of the votes cast in Paris against this "two-thirds" decree and declared it approved, the section assemblies mobilized an armed insurrection in protest.

To suppress this uprising of 13 vendémiaire IV (5 October 1795), the Convention called on troops from the regular army. This use of the army to maintain the regime set a dangerous precedent, particularly since one of the officers employed was the young general Napoleon Bonaparte, who thus brought himself to the attention of government leaders; he was rewarded with his first independent military command, which allowed him to launch his extraordinary career. Ironically, this counterrevolutionary movement aimed at restricting popular participation in politics turned out to be the last mass insurrection of the revolutionary period.

DOCUMENT J

A Justification of the Constitution of 1795

F.-A. Boissy d'Anglas had been a deputy to the National Assembly and then a moderate member of the National Convention. After the overthrow of Robespierre, he chaired the committee that drafted the socially conservative Constitution of 1795 and presented the draft to the thermidorian Convention in July 1795. In this passage, he justifies provisions that excluded the common people from voting or holding political office.

"We should be governed by the best; the best are those who are the most educated and the most interested in upholding the laws. Now, with a few exceptions, you will only find such men among those whom, being property-owners, have an attachment to the country where their property is situated, to the laws that protect it, to the tranquility that maintains it, and who owe to this property and to the advantages it gives them the education which qualifies them to discuss, with wisdom and accuracy, the pros and cons of laws that will determine the fate of their country. The man without property, on the other hand, requires a constant effort of virtue to take an interest in an order that provides him no benefits, and to oppose movements that offer him some hopes... If you give unrestricted political rights to men without property, and if they ever find themselves on the benches of the legislature, they will incite agitations or let them arise with no fear of their effects; they will impose taxes burdensome to commerce and agriculture or allow them to be imposed, because they will not have felt, or feared, or foreseen the deplorable results; and they will end up driving us into those violent convulsions from which we have just escaped, the pains of which will long be felt all over France."

(Boissy d'Anglas, *Discours préliminaire au projet de constitution pour la République française* (Paris: Imprimerie nationale, An III [1795]), 31-2. Translated by Jeremy D. Popkin.)

The Directory

The Directory has been called the only regime in France's history that never inspired any nostalgia after it fell. It has been remembered as a period of flagrant corruption, unscrupulous intrigue, and fruitless confrontation, without the dramatic high points that dominated the earlier years of the Revolution or the Napoleonic period that followed it. Recent historians have demonstrated that the Directory years were not as chaotic as this stereotype suggests. The period saw the consolidation of important institutions that continued to structure French life in the nineteenth century and saw crucial developments in the relationship between revolutionary France and its European neighbors. Perhaps the regime's greatest weakness was that it failed to inspire loyalty even among its own leaders: their betrayal led to its collapse.

The political leaders of the Directory lacked the stature of their predecessors under the National Assembly and the Convention. Paul Barras, a corrupt thermidorian Convention deputy who served on the five-man Executive Directory throughout its existence, symbolized their shortcomings. Barras had little commitment to revolutionary ideals, but he had a single-minded devotion to keeping himself and men like him in power, even at the cost of violating the republican constitution he had helped to create. Most of his fellow politicians were less disreputable than Barras. The majority were successful members of the bourgeoisie who had been active in local affairs during the early years of the Revolution. Having held public office after 1789 and often having invested in national lands, they had good reason to support the republican regime against any counterrevolution. In general, however, they had avoided taking strong positions on controversial issues prior to 1794. The result was that France was governed during the Directory years primarily by men concerned not to stick their necks out. In a crisis, these men were easily pushed aside by hardened revolutionary veterans like Barras.

Despite this weakness at the top, the Directory succeeded in restoring a certain degree of order to a country racked by six years of revolutionary upheaval. Thanks to a series of good harvests, the regime benefited from a favorable economic climate. After an unsuccessful effort to replace the worthless assignats with *mandats*, another form of paper money that also soon lost all value, the Directory in 1797 reverted to metallic currency. The Directory also resolved the government debt problem that had forced the calling of the Estates-General in 1789 and that had dogged every subsequent revolutionary government. In 1797, it "consolidated" the public debt, writing off two-thirds of it. This partial bankruptcy freed subsequent governments from a painful burden. To put the government on a sound financial footing, the Directory systematized the collection of the taxes on land and business activity imposed by the National Assembly and added new taxes on luxury items and a property tax calculated according to the number of doors and windows in each taxpayer's house. Easier to collect than the multitude of Old Regime taxes, these four taxes remained the main sources of French government revenue for a century. To enforce its policies, the Directory continued the centralization of authority begun during the Terror, sending appointed officials, called commissioners of the executive power, to oversee departmental administrations. The apparatus of the central government continued to grow throughout the period, but its increased effectiveness was masked by the government's inability to get rid of armed counterrevolutionary groups and bandit gangs in many rural areas.

An important aspect of the Directory period was the consolidation of a set of institutions that gave the country a new kind of intellectual elite. The Convention had already begun to replace the aristocratically dominated royal academies of the Old Regime with more professionally oriented institutions for research and teaching, such as the Museum of Natural History, founded in 1793, the *École normale* for teachers, and the *École polytechnique* for engineers, both set up in 1794 to teach outstanding students from all over the country. New medical schools, organized along scientific lines, were also opened that year, and the Institute, an organization intended to bring together France's leading scientists and thinkers, replaced the abolished academies in 1795. In contrast to the academies of the Old Regime, members of these new institutions were supposed to be recruited strictly on the basis of merit. In practice, they served to elevate the status of a largely bourgeois intellectual elite recruited on a national scale. Modified somewhat during the subsequent Napoleonic period, these schools and institutes formed the basis for the highly centralized educational and scientific system that still characterizes France today. The regime also tried to create new public celebrations that were not connected to the controversial political events of the Revolution. The industrial exhibition it sponsored in Paris in 1798, often seen as the ancestor of modern world's fairs, was so successful that it had to be prolonged five days beyond its planned closing date.

These new institutions served to make Paris a world center in science and medicine for the next several decades. Professors and scientists held more positions of political responsibility under the Directory than in almost any other French regime. The majority of the period's intellectuals hailed the Revolution for having cleared the way for the triumph of rationalism by its destruction of the old academies and the Church, and the Directory period saw the publication of important works that summed up the Enlightenment's worldview in a new, more rigorously scientific manner, such as the astronomer Laplace's *Exposition of the System of the World.* Leading philosophers and social thinkers formed a group known as the *Idéologues* and elaborated the science of *idéologie,* the analytic study of human thought. Taking new advances in medicine and anatomy into account, the Idéologues tried to provide a purely scientific explanation of the functioning of the mind and the laws governing human society.

Proponents of a society governed by an educated male elite, the Idéologues were unsympathetic to the lower classes and to women. Improved economic conditions took the edge off the Paris protest movements that had led to the germinal and prairial uprisings in 1795, but the regime treated the urban poor with suspicion and abandoned the social-welfare programs enacted during the Terror. In the countryside, the Directory ended the Convention's efforts to divide village common lands in favor of poor peasants, recognizing that even the law's intended beneficiaries had rarely supported it. The government sought to encourage an entrepreneurial spirit among farmers, but the agricultural advice its officials provided was poorly adapted to reality. The regime's anti-Catholic policy caused constant conflict in rural areas. Where local priests had been driven out during the Terror, laypeople, particularly women, sometimes took the initiative of restarting church services, creating a kind of popular Catholicism. The installation of a new system of conscription for the army in 1798 added to rural grievances against the republican government.

The Directory, Europe, and the Colonies

Although the Directory took some important steps to stabilize conditions inside France, its most striking achievements were military and diplomatic. Even before the fall of Robespierre, the French had regained the initiative in the war. Leading an army of former slaves, Victor Hugues drove the British out of Guadeloupe in June 1794. In the even more valuable colony of Saint-Domingue, news of the Convention's vote to abolish slavery led the most talented of the black insurgents, Toussaint Louverture, to join the French. Toussaint's black troops enabled the French to regain the initiative over the British and Spanish. Angered by Jay's Treaty, an accord that the American government had negotiated with the British in 1794, the French turned their Caribbean islands into bases for privateers that captured American ships; relationships between the two republics became steadily more acrimonious.

In Europe in the second half of 1794, the revolutionary armies swept through Belgium and the Rhineland. In the winter of 1795, they occupied the Netherlands, where they sponsored a "Batavian revolution" in which the old ruler, the Stadholder, was expelled, and a republican constitution on the French model was drawn up. The Netherlands became the first of the several "sister republics" established during the Directory period. Set up by natives of their countries, these "sister republics" rarely had a strong base of popular support and were always dependent on French military assistance. For their services in protecting the new government, the French imposed a heavy indemnity on the Dutch, a policy they repeated in other territories in the following years. The revolutionary war began to change into a war of conquest, undertaken for the profit of republican France.

France's military successes had important repercussions on the European balance of power. In April 1795, republican France and monarchist Prussia signed the Peace of Basle. The Prussians, preoccupied with an uprising in Poland and the need to limit Russian expansion there, became the first Old Regime government to treat the French Republic as a regular participant in the European state system. After the failure of their invasion of southern France and the defection of Toussaint Louverture in Saint-Domingue, the Spanish followed the Prussian example. By 1795, any expectation that foreign populations would welcome French troops as liberators had evaporated. In response, the French themselves came to treat the territories they occupied as conquests, to be exploited from the point of view of France's national interest. In October 1795, France annexed Belgium, enlarging its borders in the same way that Prussia, Austria, and Russia had by completing the partition of Poland.

Under the Directory, France continued to expand. In 1796 and 1797, French armies penetrated deep into Germany and Italy, where the young general Bonaparte scored spectacular successes, occupying the peninsula as far south as Rome. He applied the policies pioneered in the Netherlands, backing local movements to set up "sister republics," which were required to pay heavy indemnities to their liberators.

The French looted Italian churches and palaces and sent many of the country's artistic masterpieces back to Paris, outraging Italian cultural sensibilities. Such exactions alienated the local populations, which came to consider French-style reforms a smokescreen for exploitation. Anti-French uprisings in some parts of Italy and resistance to occupation in the Rhineland helped confirm the French impression that they needed to use force to keep the territories they occupied under control. But heavy-handed military rule only widened the gap between the French and the foreign populations under their domination.

France's expansion had important consequences for the army's place in French society and politics. The citizen-soldiers of 1792–1793 were now battle-hardened professionals who lost contact with the civilian population at home. The soldiers also came to have strong personal loyalties to their commanders. For their part, the leading generals became less patient with interference from the government in Paris. Financially independent because of the money they extracted from the regions their armies conquered, they developed their own policies and became important influences in domestic politics.

No other general profited more from this situation than the young commander of the Army of Italy, Napoleon Bonaparte. By the summer of 1797, with his army having crossed the Alps and threatening Vienna, the Austrians seemed ready to make peace, as Prussia had done in 1795 and Spain in 1796. Bonaparte, acting without instructions from the Directory, negotiated the treaty of Campo-Formio, in which Austria ceded its claims to Belgium and recognized the French-sponsored republics in Italy; in exchange, he offered the Austrians Venice, which his troops had conquered. This exchange of territories, carried out without any regard for their inhabitants' wishes, showed how completely France had abandoned any pretense of extending the principle of national self-determination to other peoples. In 1798, the French intervened in Switzerland, which was renamed the Helvetic Republic and added to the belt of satellite states surrounding the "Great Nation," as the French referred to themselves. In early 1799, a short-lived Parthenopean Republic replaced the Kingdom of Naples in southern Italy.

The Directory's aggressive conduct led to a rupture of relations with the United States. The "XYZ affair," in which the French foreign minister Talleyrand tried to extort bribes from the Americans, led to the "Quasi-War," an undeclared naval conflict. To put pressure on the French, the American government of John Adams aided the black general Toussaint Louverture, who was increasingly acting like an autonomous ruler in Saint-Domingue. Named commander of all French forces in the island in 1796, Toussaint outmaneuvered the various French officials sent to control him. Unable to dispatch French troops to the Caribbean because of the British naval blockade, French leaders could only watch unhappily as their most valuable colony moved to the brink of independence.

As Toussaint Louverture was gaining power in Saint-Domingue in 1798, the Directory embarked on a new kind of colonial venture in Egypt. Earlier European conquests around the world had been naked efforts to acquire land and wealth, but the French claimed that the Egyptian expedition would give the population there the benefits of progress. The idea of remaking the Middle East caught imaginations in Paris: one journalist even proposed creating a Jewish "sister republic" in Palestine, the first published plan for an independent Jewish state in modern

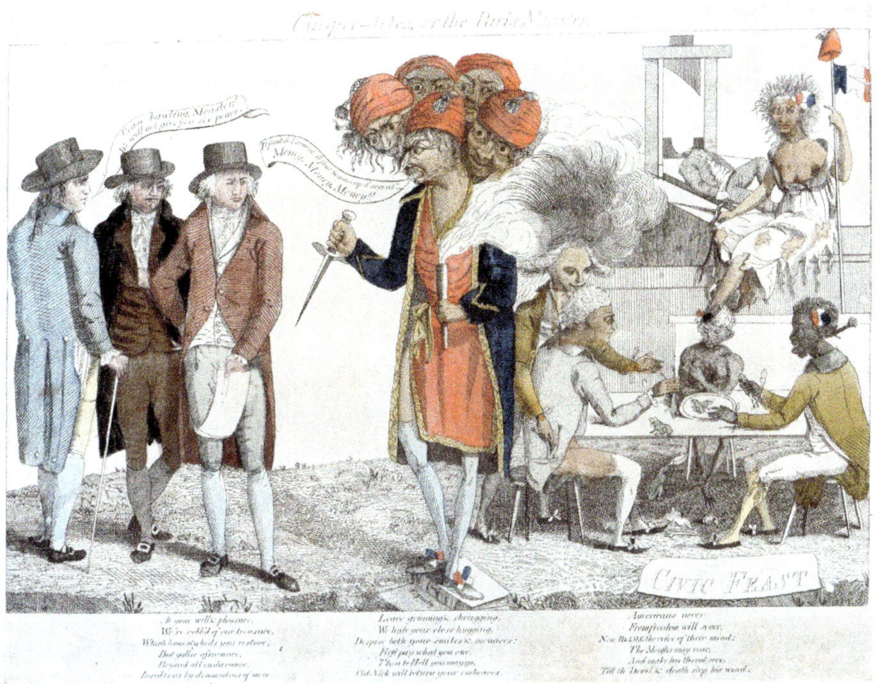

ANTI-FRENCH SENTIMENT IN THE UNITED STATES

The "XYZ Affair," in which French diplomats attempted to extort money from the American government's representatives before opening talks to resolve grievances over the seizure of American ships, led to open conflict between the two republics. In this American cartoon from 1799, the Directory is represented as a five-headed monster. The radicalism of the French Revolution—which had in fact cooled considerably by this time—was suggested by images of the guillotine, a bare-breasted woman holding a pike, and blacks joining whites in a "civic feast."

times (See Document K). Napoleon Bonaparte eagerly accepted the command of the Egyptian expedition. After landing and capturing Cairo, Bonaparte proceeded to introduce French-style institutions there. A French spokesman told the members of an assembly that Bonaparte convened that these changes would "bring justice, respect for properties, [and] enlightenment, and thereby reopen, for a people worthy of improvement, the sources of happiness." Egyptians, however, experienced the French as outsiders who ignored Islamic customs and imposed heavy taxes. Within a few months, resentment at these policies sparked an uprising in Cairo, whose brutal repression further alienated the population. When French troops invaded the great mosque of Al-Azhar, "they treated the books and Qur'anic volumes as trash, throwing them on the ground... They guzzled wine and smashed the bottles in the central court," an Egyptian chronicler reported.[1] The many scientists who accompanied the expedition founded the modern study of Egyptian antiquity—among their discoveries was the Rosetta stone, whose inscriptions unlocked the secret of Egyptian hieroglyphs—but Napoleon's invasion was also the start of a clash of cultures that still affects the world today.

DOCUMENT K

French Policy, "Sister Republics," and the Jews

The Directory encouraged the formation of "sister republics" that would support French interests and help finance France's expansionist foreign policy. This "Letter of a Jew to His Brethren," published in a Paris newspaper in 1798 at the moment when Napoleon's expedition to Egypt was focusing interest on the Middle East, shows this policy being adapted to the situation of Europe's Jewish minority. Nothing came of the proposal at the time, but the "Letter," even though it was probably written by a French propagandist who was not Jewish, is the first modern proposal for the creation of a Jewish national state.

"It is time to reclaim our place among the nations... An invincible nation that fills the world with its glory has shown us what patriotism can do. Let us beg for its generosity, let us ask for its aid, and be assured that the philosophy that guides the leaders of this sublime nation, will make them accept our request.... A council will be set up, whose members will be elected by the Jews scattered in Europe, in Asia, in Africa... The council will offer the French government, if it gives us the aid we will need to return to our fatherland and maintain ourselves, (1) financial compensation; (2) to share with French merchants *exclusively* the trade with the Indies."

(Source: *Ami des lois*, 20 prairial An VI [7 June 1798]. Translated by Jeremy D. Popkin.)

The "Politics of the Balance"

Although it expanded French power abroad, the Directory could not achieve political stability at home. The vendémiaire uprising in October 1795 showed that the new regime could not trust the middle-class property owners to whom the constitution-makers of 1795 had tried to appeal. Many of them had been deeply shaken by the Terror and remained hostile to the republican government. They supported politicians who hinted broadly at the restoration of the monarchy and a purge of all those who had held important political positions during the radical phase of the Revolution. On the other hand, a significant number of former Jacobins remained politically active, denouncing the Directory government for being insufficiently dedicated to the principles of liberty and equality. The religious issue remained divisive: militant republicans and Idéologue intellectuals continued to identify Catholicism with counterrevolution and obscurantism, whereas the faithful denounced the regime's restrictions on worship and religious education.

Rather than following a clear policy in either direction, the government of the Directory initially strove to appear above politics. It followed a "balance-beam policy" of alternating blows against the royalists and the neo-Jacobins. In May 1796, the government attacked the radical left. It arrested the agitator Gracchus Babeuf, an agrarian radical who advocated communal ownership of property, along with a number of former supporters of Robespierre. Babeuf had absorbed the lesson of the defeated sans-culotte uprisings in 1795, concluding that the regime could not be overthrown by a spontaneous popular insurrection. Instead, he tried to organize a conspiracy to overthrow the Directory and install a dictatorship that would carry out his communist program. His plan never had much chance of success, but his arrest presented the Directory with a chance to pose as the firm defender of social order and the rights of property. The arrest of a group of royalist conspirators in February 1797 allowed the government to show that it was equally opposed to any return of the Old Regime.

Rather than rewarding the Directory for its balanced policy, voters in the first regular parliamentary elections in April 1797 elected conservative deputies who promised to continue the purge of politicians who had supported the radical phase of the Revolution. The conservatives, who debated their policies at the "Club de Clichy" and were known as the "Clichyens," also promised to restore the rights of white property owners in France's colonies. Divided about whether to work for a constitutional monarchy or to achieve what they could within the republican constitution, the conservatives spent the summer of 1797 arguing among themselves. The five-man Directory was also divided. Two of its members favored an attempt to work with the more moderate Clichyens. The other three, led by Barras, rejected this idea and decided to use force to halt the spread of counterrevolutionary tendencies.

The pro-republican "triumvirate," headed by Barras, arranged for military support. From Italy, Napoleon Bonaparte sent one of his generals to command the troops used to back the plan and had his soldiers sign proclamations threatening to march on Paris if the right-wing election results were allowed to stand. On 18 fructidor V (4 September 1797), Barras and his colleagues staged a coup, expelling their two more moderate colleagues from the Directory, purging the prominent right-wing deputies from the Councils, and banning more than thirty daily papers. Despite ample warning, the right-wing deputies and journalists put up no resistance and received no popular support. They had attempted to use the legal means provided by the 1795 constitution to undermine the regime; they failed to understand that their republican opponents would resort to force to keep themselves in power.

The "Second Directory"

The fructidor coup marked a turning point in the Directory's policies. The "Second Directory" abandoned the "balance-beam" tactics used in 1795–1797 and reverted to the militant republican rhetoric of 1793. Pro-government deputies clamored (unsuccessfully) for a law expelling all former nobles from the country, and the government did take drastic measures against "refractory" Catholic priests, many of whom had been quietly allowed to resume their posts after thermidor. To suppress crime and disorder in the provinces, the government put large areas under a "state of siege," suspending normal court procedures. A new national police force, the *gendarmerie*, was expanded to help maintain order. The Second Directory also intensified efforts to spread the new republican culture. It enforced the celebration of the *décadi,* the tenth day of the republican week according to the new calendar, in place of Sunday, and encouraged writers like the poet Évariste Parny, whose *La Guerre des Dieux* ("The War of the Gods") ridiculed Christian beliefs in elegant but often blasphemous lyrics. Outside France, the Second Directory encouraged fructidor-style coups in the "sister republics" that turned their policies in a more radical direction. It also promised to make the populations of its overseas colonies full French citizens, regardless of their race. Recognizing that war had become a virtually permanent feature of the country's life, the Second Directory introduced a regular system of conscription to replenish the army's ranks, which were still filled with men who had volunteered or been drafted in the crisis atmosphere of 1793. The system set up by the Jourdan law of 1798 would enable Napoleon to build up the army with which he would try to conquer all of Europe.

The new atmosphere encouraged the militant republicans, or neo-Jacobins, who scored important gains in the elections of April 1798. But the Directory was no more willing to have its policies shaped by an autonomous neo-Jacobin movement than it had been to accept the influence of the conservatives elected in 1797. It responded by "correcting" the voters' decisions in the coup of 22 floréal VI (11 May 1798), installing its own backers in contested races. The fructidor and floréal coups showed that political power had become concentrated in the hands of a group of professional politicians whom French historian Pierre Serna has called men of the "extreme center." Supported by most of the Idéologue intellectuals, they were willing to use authoritarian tactics to keep both conservatives and radicals out of power. Many of them openly argued that France needed a government with a stronger executive branch than that provided by the Directory.

Whether a regime with such a narrow base of support could have survived thanks to economic prosperity and military success is hard to say. But the Directory was certainly poorly placed to cope with a crisis, and, by the end of 1798, it was confronting one. A new foreign coalition had assembled against France. It included the British, the Austrians, who hoped to reverse the unfavorable treaty of Campo-Formio of 1797, and the Russians, whose new ruler, Tsar Paul, harbored a fanatical hatred for the Revolution. In the first half of 1799, the French armies were defeated on every front. This sudden military collapse discredited the Directory at home. The Directors once again failed to control the spring parliamentary elections, and a broad coalition of discontented deputies reversed the procedure of the coups of fructidor and floréal, purging the Directory itself in the coup of 30 prairial VII (18 June 1799).

The Fall of the Directory

The prairial victors came from two very different camps. Some were neo-Jacobins who believed that the military crisis required a revival of the emergency measures and the patriotic spirit of 1793. Others, led by Sieyès, who was now a member of the Directory, intended to "revise" the Constitution of 1795 so that it would no longer be vulnerable to periodic challenges from either right or left. At first, the neo-Jacobins seemed to hold the upper hand. They pushed through a forced loan to levy money from the rich, and the "law of hostages," which allowed local officials to deal with counterrevolutionary unrest by arresting relatives of nobles and émigrés. These measures revived unhappy memories of the Terror and provoked considerable resistance. Meanwhile, Sieyès and his group conspired to rid themselves of their neo-Jacobin allies. Recognizing their lack of organized public support, the plotters looked for a popular military figure to serve as their figurehead.

As Sieyès was casting around for a suitable general, the most celebrated of the Directory's commanders unexpectedly reappeared in Paris. Having learned of France's defeats in Europe and alarmed by letters about his wife's infidelities,

Napoleon Bonaparte abandoned his army in Egypt and arrived in France at the beginning of October. Large crowds turned out to cheer him as he traveled from the Mediterranean to Paris; his remarkable military accomplishments had made him genuinely popular. Napoleon had long since given up the revolutionary radicalism that had once made him a friend of Robespierre's younger brother and had led to his arrest after thermidor. He quickly cast his lot with the Sieyès group, who arranged for his appointment as commander of the troops in Paris. In three weeks, the coup plan was completed; on 18 brumaire VIII (9 November 1799), it was put into effect.

Deputies sympathetic to the plotters invoked a constitutional provision allowing the legislature to convene outside Paris in case of a crisis. By the time the two Councils met in the Parisian suburb of Saint-Cloud on 19 brumaire, however, many deputies had become suspicious of the claim that there was an emergency. When Napoleon Bonaparte addressed the Council of 500, members accused him of seeking to become dictator. The shaken general retreated from the meeting hall, and the entire plan threatened to collapse. It was saved by Napoleon's younger brother Lucien, who persuaded the soldiers surrounding the legislators to intervene. Most of the deputies fled. Those who remained voted to give full powers to Sieyès and his group to prepare a new constitution. The members of the Directory were pressured into resigning. The lack of public reaction showed how little support the Directory had had.

Critical Thinking Questions

1. The overthrow of Robespierre and the radical Jacobins on 9 thermidor Year II (27 July 1794) had important political and social consequences. List the major changes that followed the thermidorians' victory. Why are these changes often described as a reaction against the principles of liberty and equality?
2. During the years from 1794 to 1799, the armies of republican France won major victories and greatly expanded the country's territory. Explain the consequences of this military expansion for the Revolution, at home and abroad.
3. Even though it brought relative stability to France, the Directory was an unpopular regime. Analyze the reasons for its lack of public support. Do they reflect a broader turning away from the Revolution's ideals of liberty and equality?

Note

1. François Pairault, *Gaspard Monge, le fondateur de Polytechnique* (Paris: Taillander, 2000), 373; *Napoleon in Egypt: Al-Jabarti's Chronicle of the French Occupation*, 1798, trans. Shmuel Moreh (Princeton, N.J.: Markus Weiner Publishing, 1975), 93.

CHAPTER 7

The Napoleonic Consulate, 1799–1804

LEARNING OBJECTIVES

After studying this chapter, you will be able to:

- **Explain the major features of the government Napoleon created during the Consulate period.**
- **Analyze the reasons why most of the French population accepted Napoleon's regime.**
- **Debate whether Napoleon continued the Revolution or ended it.**

The plotters who overthrew the Directory in November 1799 claimed to be protecting the achievements of the Revolution. For the first five years after the brumaire coup, France officially remained a republic. The motto "Liberty and Equality" continued to appear on coins and government documents, and the country was largely governed by men who had established their careers since 1789. But it quickly became obvious that the brumaire coup had produced a fundamental change. The participatory politics inaugurated in 1789, already robbed of much of its substance, first by the Jacobins, then by the Directory, disappeared, and one man concentrated all real power in his own hands.

From 1799 until his coronation as Emperor in 1804, Napoleon Bonaparte held the title of First Consul, and the regime was known as the Consulate. Whereas the Directory has been remembered in French history as ineffective and disreputable, the period of the Consulate has often been seen as one of the most brilliant eras in the country's history. Profiting from the unpopularity of the preceding regime, Bonaparte silenced the warring political factions of the previous decade. He oversaw the creation of an efficient administrative machine, consolidated many of the achievements of the Revolution, ended the conflict with the Catholic Church, and compelled all of France's enemies to make peace on favorable terms. Critics of Napoleon pointed out, however, that these accomplishments were achieved by abandoning the revolutionary movement's goal of a government based on genuine popular participation and by curtailing many of the liberties enshrined in the Declaration of the Rights of Man. More recently, modern

OPPOSITION TO NAPOLEON

Napoleon faced considerable opposition during the early years of his reign. Republican loyalists criticized his abandonment of revolutionary principles, while royalists still longed for the return of the Bourbons. In December 1800, royalist conspirators attempted to assassinate the First Consul by detonating a large explosive charge concealed in a wagon as his carriage passed by, thus inventing the modern terrorist tactic of car bombing. Napoleon seized the occasion to punish not only the perpetrators but also a number of former revolutionaries.

historians have stressed the many continuities between the preceding revolutionary regimes, especially the Directory, and the Consulate. Many of the achievements Napoleon claimed credit for had in fact been initiated before he took power.

The Consul and the Consulate

The coup of 18 brumaire, which brought Napoleon Bonaparte to power, was more the work of Sieyès, the veteran politician who had done so much to launch the Revolution ten years earlier, than of the man who reaped the main benefit from it. Sieyès's intentions were the same as those of the authors of the 1795 constitution: to consolidate the power of moderate republican politicians and bourgeois property holders and to prevent any revival of either royalism or Jacobinism. To achieve this, Sieyès planned to abolish the parliamentary elections that had troubled the Directory so much. Instead, he proposed a system of co-optation, in which politicians already in power would pick their own successors from lists of property-owning "notables" drawn up by local electoral assemblies. Before Sieyès could implement his ideas, however, he had to negotiate with the young general he had been forced to bring into his coup plan. He quickly discovered that Napoleon Bonaparte had definite ideas of his own about how France should be governed. The rest of France soon learned the same lesson.

More has been written about Napoleon Bonaparte than about any other figure in France's long history. He has been hailed as a political and military genius and condemned as the first modern totalitarian dictator, credited with consolidating the achievements of the Revolution and damned for destroying it. In the nineteenth century, with its cult of romantic genius, Napoleon was often seen as a colossus, a unique figure who changed the course of his era. More recent historians have tended to downplay both his personal impact and the importance of the changes that occurred in France during the fifteen years of his rule. Regardless of how one evaluates the impact of Napoleon's reign, however, he has certainly haunted France's collective memory. The "Napoleonic legend," planted in Napoleon's own propaganda and memoirs and cultivated by a host of subsequent artists, historians, and writers, has been a major aspect of French culture.

Napoleon's Career

Napoleon, it has often been said, was a "child of the Revolution," who owed his rise to the upheaval of 1789. Born in 1769 to a minor noble family on the island of Corsica, a territory annexed to France just a year earlier, the young Bonaparte learned to regard politics as a struggle among rival clans. Sent to cadet school on the mainland, he impressed teachers and fellow cadets with his intelligence and fierce willpower, but because of his modest background, his prospects for promotion in the prerevolutionary army were not dazzling. A young lieutenant of artillery at the time of the Revolution, he enthusiastically embraced its promise of "careers open to talent."

The emigration of many aristocratic army officers after 1789 and the outbreak of war in 1792 turned those possibilities into realities. Napoleon's skillful use of artillery in the campaign against the federalist rebels in Toulon in 1793 won the day for the Convention's forces and brought him promotion to the rank of general. Augustin Robespierre, a deputy on mission in the area and the younger brother of the Montagnard leader, became his patron and had him draft plans for an invasion of Italy. As a result of this association, Napoleon nearly fell victim to the purge that followed 9 thermidor. Briefly imprisoned, he remained unemployed until the Convention called on him for help in putting down the counterrevolutionary uprising of 13 vendémiaire in October 1795. This gained him entry to Barras's political circle, where he met and hastily married Josephine Beauharnais, the widow of an aristocrat executed during the Terror. As a reward for his services on 13 vendémiaire, he was given command of the French army in Italy, a secondary front that had not attracted much attention.

In the Italian campaign of 1796, Napoleon immediately demonstrated the qualities that were to carry him to glory. With his determined personality, he succeeded in inspiring his troops and imposing his authority on subordinate officers who were often older and more experienced than he was. He had a remarkable ability to sense the decisive point where victory could be obtained, and then acting boldly to achieve it. Outnumbered by the combined Austrian and Piedmontese forces opposing him, Bonaparte lured his foes into fighting him separately. In two months, he knocked the Piedmontese out of the war, chased the Austrians from Milan, and established himself as the most brilliant of the French Republic's generals. As commander of the French occupation forces in northern Italy, he showed himself an adept politician as well. He stage-managed the creation of carefully controlled sister republics, enriched both himself and the Directory from the levies he raised, and successfully courted the Catholic Church, avoiding the religious conflicts that had dogged the Revolution at home.

The Directory recognized Bonaparte's driving ambition and kept him at arm's length after he negotiated his own peace treaty with the Austrians in 1797. Inspired by memories of the glory that great conquerors like Alexander had won in the Middle East, Bonaparte eagerly took on the command of the expedition to Egypt in 1798. Cut off from France by the British navy after the destruction of his ships at the battle of Aboukir following his landing, he lost touch with Paris politics and only belatedly learned about the military defeats of the first half of 1799. Together with worries about his wife Josephine's infidelities, reported in letters from his brothers, the fear that the Republic might collapse and destroy his own career prompted Bonaparte to abandon his army in Egypt and sail back to France.

The Institutions of the Consulate

On arriving in Paris, Bonaparte quickly realized that his popularity gave him the chance to play a major political role. But the planning for the brumaire coup was largely carried out by Sieyès and his allies, and Bonaparte's stumbling performance in front of the Council of 500 at Saint-Cloud on 19 brumaire led many to underestimate his political ability. As the successful plotters set out to remake the constitution, Sieyès intended to shunt Bonaparte aside with a high-sounding title but little real power. But the general quickly showed that he had more political acumen than his performance on 19 brumaire had suggested.

In the negotiations about the details of the new constitution, Bonaparte proved more than a match for Sieyès. He was unconcerned with most of the document's details—a constitution, he remarked, should be "short and obscure"—but he insisted that real power, instead of being carefully divided, should be concentrated in the hands of a single official. He accepted those parts of Sieyès's draft that weakened parliamentary government, as well as the elimination of a declaration of rights such as the three previous revolutionary constitutions had contained. But he insisted on the creation of a strong executive branch, headed by three Consuls. The First Consul was to have much greater powers than his two colleagues and, in case of a disagreement among them, his decision would prevail. Once Bonaparte's definition of the First Consul's role was accepted, it was inevitable that he would be entrusted with the office; no one else had the prestige and popularity to fill it. Two minor political figures were appointed as the other Consuls, and Sieyès was relegated to the presidency of the largely powerless Senate that he had designed.

The brumairian plotters submitted this hastily drafted Constitution of the Year VIII to a vote, or plebiscite, in which all adult men were allowed to participate, in contrast to the Directory's restrictions on political participation. This enabled Bonaparte to maintain that he had a democratic mandate to govern. Votes were not secret, however, and only 1,500 citizens risked identifying themselves as opponents of the new regime. Government officials were ordered to pad the totals to make the plebiscite look like a success. France was weary of political turmoil and disenchanted with revolutionary ideals, but it remained up to Bonaparte to show that he could do better.

Consolidation of Power

To consolidate his power, the new First Consul, increasingly referred to as Napoleon, rather than by his family name, moved quickly to break up the political factions created by the Revolution. He muzzled the political press and used the police to harass prominent neo-Jacobins and die-hard royalists. But all those political figures between the extremes were welcomed into the system. By choosing collaborators regardless of their attitude to the Revolution, Napoleon did much to defuse the bitter conflicts of the previous decade.

A key feature of the Napoleonic system was the establishment of a streamlined government that could act swiftly and effectively. Napoleon strengthened the already centralized bureaucracy by the creation of the prefects, administrators appointed in Paris and dispatched to the departments to oversee local administration. The prefects bore some resemblance to the prerevolutionary intendants and to the Directory's commissioners, but they had more extensive powers in the field, while being more strictly controlled from Paris. Thanks to the Revolution, they faced no institutional opposition in their local regions: the reforms of 1789 had abolished all the traditional privileged bodies that had obstructed the monarchy's officials. Appointed from Paris and rotated from post to post after a few years to keep them from becoming attached to local interests, the prefects, who were drawn from a variety of political backgrounds, gave the central government a powerful mechanism for imposing its will on the country.

The laws the prefects enforced were no longer the result of stormy public legislative debates, as they had been during the Revolution. Napoleon concentrated real lawmaking powers in a new body, the *Conseil d'Etat,* or Council of State, in which he often participated personally. The Conseil's meetings were held in secret. Napoleon appointed competent and articulate councillors drawn, like the prefects, from diverse political camps, whom he allowed to engage in free-wheeling debate. Once he had approved a proposed law, however, public debates were largely a formality. The deputies, divided under Sieyès's complicated scheme into a Tribunate, which debated proposals without voting on them, a Legislative Body, which listened to the debates and voted without speaking, and a Senate supposedly charged with preventing violations of the constitution, generally accepted the government's proposals.

With all real power in his own hands and with the new administrative and lawmaking machinery under his control, Napoleon was able to govern more effectively than any previous French ruler. To carry out his wishes, he recruited a talented team of ministers. Charles Gaudin served as finance minister throughout Napoleon's reign, successfully keeping the government out of the fiscal problems that had plagued the Old Regime. Napoleon's loyal companion Alexander Berthier oversaw the army, and Jean-Antoine Chaptal held the key post of minister of the interior. In foreign affairs, the ex-bishop Talleyrand retained the office he had held during the Directory, while the efficient but ruthless ex-terrorist Fouché managed the police.

Under this leadership, the campaign against rural disorder, begun under the Directory, was intensified, with "flying columns" of troops and gendarmes turning suspects over to special military courts for quick punishment. During the 1790s, local populations had often sympathized with resistance to the government for political reasons. As Napoleon's message that the quarrels of the Revolution were over sank in, peasants became more willing to assist the forces of order. When he thought he was facing political opposition, Napoleon could be as ruthless as any of the earlier revolutionary leaders. After an unsuccessful attempt on his life in December 1800, he ordered the deportation of over one hundred former revolutionary militants, an order he maintained even after his police officials proved that the plot against him was actually the work of royalist conspirators. Napoleon's repressive measures ensured that there would be no resurgence of the popular revolutionary and counterrevolutionary violence that had such an important feature of the revolutionary decade. The Napoleonic "security state," as historian Howard Brown has called it, achieved a monopoly on the use of violence. Most of the population accepted the situation, grateful for an end to the troubles of the revolutionary period.

The economic revival that had begun under the Directory continued under the Consulate, benefiting merchants and manufacturers and providing jobs for workers. The establishment of the Bank of France in 1800 made it easier for the government to borrow money while also supplying credit for private business needs. In 1803, the new government completed the restabilization of France's currency begun under the Directory by issuing new gold coins. These "gold Napoleons" remained the standard of value in France for over a century. Napoleon reassured the purchasers of the national lands sold under the Revolution that their acquisitions would be protected, even though he allowed many of the émigrés whose estates had been confiscated and sold to return to the country. This "Napoleonic settlement," under which properties and positions attained during the Revolution were guaranteed in exchange for acceptance of Napoleon's one-man rule, satisfied most of the population. The spy network set up by Fouché kept the others under surveillance.

Napoleon's policies and the efficient government he established did much to make his regime successful, but his personality also played an essential part in this process. Able to grasp complex issues quickly, Napoleon held his own in discussions with intellectuals and experts in a wide variety of fields. In personal conversations, he could exert a magnetic charm. In dealing with his ministers, Napoleon made sure that his wishes were carried out and kept the behind-the-scenes intrigues that had characterized the Bourbon monarchy to a minimum. Particularly in the Consulate years, his youth and energy made a striking contrast to the indecisiveness of Louis XVI and the apparent ineffectiveness of most revolutionary politicians.

The Peace of Amiens and the Concordat

To complete his policy of liquidating the conflicts engendered by the Revolution, Napoleon needed to resolve two crucial issues: the foreign war and the religious struggle. Even before the brumaire coup, the French armies had stopped the Coalition's advances, but France had lost much of the territory gained under the Directory. The Russians quarreled with their allies and withdrew from the war, allowing Napoleon to turn his attention to defeating Austria. Leaving Paris behind before his new regime was fully consolidated, he headed for Italy, taking personal control of a newly formed army at Dijon. With Austrian forces tied down by a lengthy siege at Genoa, Napoleon saw a chance to surprise them from the rear. He led his forces through the narrow Alpine passes, and in June 1800, his dramatic victory at Marengo restored French control of northern Italy. Sieyès and the Idéologue circle in Paris had barely concealed their hopes that a military defeat would make him vulnerable and end his plan to establish one-man rule. The Marengo victory ended their chance of undermining him. The Austrians continued the fight on the German front, but General Moreau's victory at Hohenlinden in southern Germany in December 1800 forced them to accept the treaty of Lunéville in February 1801, giving France even greater gains than the 1797 Campo-Formio agreement. France now annexed the German territories west of the Rhine River that it had occupied since 1795, setting in motion a reshuffling of borders throughout the Holy Roman Empire as rulers who had lost lands to France were given compensation elsewhere. Regimes loyal to Napoleon replaced the "sister republics" in the Netherlands and the Italian peninsula.

With Austria out of the war, Britain made overtures for peace as well. In the treaty signed at Amiens in March 1802, Britain made a few colonial gains but had to acknowledge France's continental predominance. With this treaty, Napoleon appeared to have brought the war begun in 1792 to a glorious conclusion. He could boast that revolutionary France had expanded far beyond the limits dreamed of by its Bourbon kings; the other European powers had had to recognize France's "natural frontiers" along the crest of the Alps and the Rhine River.

Napoleon's enthusiasm for the Egyptian expedition had shown his personal interest in overseas colonies. He was unable to rescue the French troops stranded in Egypt, who finally surrendered to the British in 1801, but the Peace of Amiens allowed him to try to reassert French control over its Caribbean colonies. As part of the treaty, Britain returned the island of Martinique, where the 1794 decree abolishing slavery had never been implemented. Former plantation owners lobbied Napoleon to reimpose slavery in the other sugar islands, Guadeloupe and Saint-Domingue. Large military expeditions were sent to the French colonies in early 1802, and a law passed in May 1802 repealed the Convention's 1794 decree abolishing slavery. Later that year, Napoleon required all blacks living in France to register with the police.

In Guadeloupe, the French expedition succeeded, at the price of extensive bloodshed. In the larger colony of Saint-Domingue, General Victor Leclerc also achieved initial successes. Toussaint Louverture, who had brought the island to the brink of independence, was arrested and shipped to France, and his leading generals submitted to the French. Leclerc soon found himself facing guerrilla resistance in the countryside, however, and he lost many of his troops to yellow fever, which killed the general himself in November 1802. In the last weeks before he died, Leclerc had warned Napoleon that the war could only be won by resorting to genocidal measures. "We must destroy all the Negroes in the mountains…and not leave in the colony a single man of color who has worn an officer's epaulette," he wrote.[1] The black officers who had joined the French defected to the rebels; one of them, Jean-Jacques Dessalines, became the new leader of the black struggle. After war with England resumed in 1803, Leclerc's successor Rochambeau was cut off from reinforcements. Despite resorting to extremely brutal tactics, he finally had to surrender. Dessalines proclaimed the colony as the independent nation of Haiti. The Leclerc expedition cost the French more than 50,000 troops; it was Napoleon's worst defeat until the debacles in Spain and Russia during the Empire. As he realized that defeat in Saint-Domingue was unavoidable, Napoleon decided to offer the United States France's claims to its territories in North America through the Louisiana Purchase arrangement of 1803; he hoped to keep these lands out of the hands of the British or Spanish. The success of the Haitian insurrection thus set the stage for the rise of the United States to the status of a continental power.

At the same time as he negotiated with Britain in 1801, Napoleon had undertaken efforts to resolve the split between the Revolution and the Church. Napoleon had no firm religious beliefs of his own. In Egypt, he had made a great show of courting Muslim leaders. But he considered religion a useful instrument of social control. "How can there be any order in a State without religion? Society cannot exist without inequality of fortune, and inequality of fortune cannot exist without religion," he once remarked.[2] He was also determined to end the conflict that had grown out of the Revolution's religious reform efforts. His strategy was to go over the heads of the counterrevolutionary French bishops, most of whom had gone into exile during the 1790s, and deal directly with the Pope, Pius VII, a man who had shown some sympathy for revolutionary reforms during Napoleon's first occupation of Italy.

Negotiations for a *Concordat,* or treaty, between the French government and the Papacy were successfully completed in July 1801. The agreement recognized Catholicism as the religion of the majority of the population and allowed the resumption of public worship. The government would pay priests and bishops; as under the Old Regime, it would nominate bishops, who would receive their consecration from the Pope. To end the schism resulting from the Civil Constitution, the Pope called on all French bishops, both émigrés and constitutionals who had remained in France, to submit their resignations and appointed a new hierarchy including members of both factions. The Church had to accept the permanent loss of its confiscated lands and the legalization of other religions, as well as government control of higher education and tight regulation of religious orders and charitable activities. Napoleon unilaterally added regulations known as the "Organic Articles" to the Concordat before its publication, giving the government almost complete control over the internal administration of the Church. Napoleon's behavior foretold future conflicts, but the reopening of churches and the opportunity to replace long-absent priests permitted Catholicism to begin reestablishing its position in French life.

Many prominent ex-revolutionaries objected to the Concordat and blamed Napoleon for abandoning the Revolution's hard-won triumph over what they saw as outmoded superstition. But the majority of the population welcomed the end of the conflict that had begun with the imposition of the Civil Constitution of the Clergy. The Protestant and Jewish religious minorities still enjoyed the legal protection they had been granted after 1789. In 1806, Napoleon took the extraordinary step of convoking an international congress of Jewish religious leaders, the Sanhedrin, to clarify the relationship between French and Jewish law. Together with the granting of citizenship rights to Jews in 1791, the meeting of the Sanhedrin constituted a remarkable departure in the relations between Jews and the world around them, and not even Napoleon's imposition of discriminatory regulations on Jewish moneylenders of Alsace in 1808 destroyed the impression made by his earlier initiative.

To round out the changes made to consolidate his regime, in May 1802, Napoleon announced the creation of the Legion of Honor, an award to be given to those who had rendered outstanding service to the country. Giving special distinctions to certain citizens struck many as a violation of the Revolution's promise of equality, but Napoleon maintained that he was not creating a new privileged class. Membership was not hereditary, and any French citizen could earn the coveted cross. To critics of his reliance on "baubles" instead of devotion to the public good, Napoleon responded that "it is with 'baubles' that mankind is governed."[3] The Peace of Amiens, the Concordat, and the successful restoration of domestic order brought Napoleon to the height of his popularity. In a plebiscite in late 1802, more than three-and-one-half million voters approved Napoleon's being named First Consul for life; only 8,000 cast negative votes.

The introduction of a new civil law code, known as the *Code Napoléon,* in 1804, gave the new individualistic and family-based society created during the Revolution a permanent basis. Since 1792, France's revolutionary legislators had labored to replace the hundreds of prerevolutionary local law codes with a single national system. The project, carried to completion at Napoleon's urging, implemented a conservative version of the Revolution's major principles at the level of everyday life. It gave property owners the clear right to use their wealth as they saw fit, eliminating the last vestiges of feudal dues on land and guild restrictions on business. In the interests of equality, revolutionary legislators had required parents to divide their property equally among their children, outlawing the system of primogeniture that had kept estates intact before the Revolution. The Civil Code retreated on this point, allowing one privileged heir to receive an extra portion of parental property. The Code's harsh restrictions on women's rights reflected a male-dominated vision of the family: husbands had full control of their family's property and the fate of their children. Women who married foreigners lost their French citizenship. Divorce was sharply restricted, though not completely abolished, and the husband had greater latitude to start proceedings than the wife, whereas the 1792 law had treated men and women equally. Although its provisions about women's rights have been modified, the Civil Code still remains the basis of French civil law today. Introduced in many territories the French occupied during the Napoleonic era, and adopted in the state of Louisiana, it proved to be one of the most influential results of the French Revolution.

Elements of Opposition

As long as Napoleon marched from victory to victory, there was little visible opposition to him at home. Under the surface, however, there was quiet resistance to the regime's increasing authoritarianism. Napoleon could hire artists to glorify him and pamphleteers to praise him, but he was unable to win over the country's major thinkers. The leading members of the rationalist Idéologue group that had formed during the Directory period became the hard core of the opposition to him during the Consulate. Convinced that republican institutions reflected the dictates of reason, the Ideologues and politicians close to them objected to Napoleon's subversion of legislative autonomy, his abolition of genuine elections, and his restoration of slavery and the Catholic Church.

In 1802, Napoleon eliminated the Idéologues' supporters from the legislative councils, and, in 1803, he suppressed their institutional stronghold, the Third Section of the Institute, but he remained uneasily aware of their silent disapproval of the regime. Paris continued to be a center of scientific activity, but imperial policy favored applied research over theoretical investigations, and leadership in many fields began to shift to the less restricted universities in Germany. Napoleon maintained the grandes écoles, such as the École polytechnique, set up during the revolutionary decade to train the nation's intellectual elite, but he imposed a quasi-military discipline that independent-minded students like the future romantic poet Victor Hugo resented.

Napoleon himself thought that he might find support among the thinkers associated with the revival of Catholicism that had begun even before the Concordat. As a result of the controversy over the Civil Constitution of the Clergy and the de-Christianizers' attacks on the Church, those priests who lacked a real commitment to the faith had left the Church. Those who stayed formed a clergy far more serious about its beliefs than the common run of their prerevolutionary predecessors. The laity's faith had also been renewed. During the Terror, many formerly free-thinking nobles and other victims of persecution had embraced Catholicism, and many of the émigrés had found consolation in religion during their years in exile. One of them, François-René de Chateaubriand, captured this mood of religious revival in his two-volume *Genius of Christianity,* which appeared in April 1802, just at the moment of the first Easter celebration in Paris's Notre-Dame Cathedral since 1793. Chateaubriand's lyrical evocation of religion's aesthetic and emotional appeal made Catholicism fashionable, particularly among the upper classes, who had frequently distanced themselves from it before 1789. The success of Chateaubriand's book marked a shift in the intellectual climate. As another defender of Catholicism wrote, the experience of the Revolution had discredited the anti-religious philosophers of the Enlightenment. "Their brilliant fantasies dissolved when an attempt was made to realize them; their principles, so sublime in theory, turned out in practice to be disastrous dreams."[4] Chateaubriand marked a break with the Enlightenment not only because of his embrace of Catholicism but also because of his emphasis on the superiority of emotion over reason. He was one of the first writers of the French romantic movement; his novel *René* was one of the first to sound the characteristic romantic themes of introspection and melancholy. These themes were prominent in the work of the numerous women writers whose sentimental novels were among the great publishing successes of the Consulate years. Works such as Madame de Staël's *Delphine* featured heroines misunderstood and rejected by a stiflingly conformist society. The popularity of these novels showed that many women were still dissatisfied with their place in French society, even if they eschewed the public demonstrations of the early revolutionary years.

Like the romantic artists, the social thinkers of the period were united only by their distaste for the imperial regime. The thinkers of the Idéologue tradition continued to defend the rationalist individualism of the Enlightenment, implicitly condemning the Concordat and the increasingly rigid controls on intellectual activity. The economist Jean-Baptiste Say was a typical representative of this tradition. His *Treatise of Political Economy,* published in 1803, adapted and systematized Adam Smith's doctrines of economic liberty, which were in sharp contrast to Napoleon's policies of state intervention.

More original was the conservative Catholic thinker Louis de Bonald. During his years as an émigré, this provincial nobleman had elaborated a far-reaching critique of rationalism and individualism, which he blamed for the horrors of the Revolution. He argued that society needed an unquestioned principle of authority, which he found in the Catholic Church. The truth of its doctrines was confirmed, he argued, by the testimony of tradition. A body of beliefs that had endured for 1,800 years was more reliable than the speculations of modern philosophers. Society, according to Bonald, was a living organism that needed to be governed by a single head, not an agreement among private individuals. Until France returned to a society in accordance with divine will, with authority flowing from God through the Pope and the king to the aristocracy and finally down to the common people, it would continue to be racked by turmoil. Bonald's organic conception of society made him one of the ancestors of modern sociology. The authoritarian cast of his doctrines attracted Napoleon, but he could not wean the stubborn marquis away from his loyalty to the Bourbon monarchy.

Bonald was only one of a number of writers who contributed to the revival of royalist sentiment under the Empire. He and many others contributed occasional articles to the *Journal des Débats,* the most widely read newspaper of the period, whose sympathy for the Bourbon monarchy was barely disguised. Unable to raise the issue directly, the paper's contributors turned to literary and theatrical criticism, condemning the writings of Voltaire and the philosophes and glorifying the classic seventeenth-century works of Corneille and Racine, with their royal heroes. The popularity of this thinly veiled royalist propaganda continued to remind Napoleon that he had not achieved a solid grip on educated French public opinion.

Critical Thinking Questions

1. After seizing power in 1799, Napoleon Bonaparte established a new government that proved much more successful than the short-lived revolutionary regimes it replaced. Describe the major features of the Napoleonic regime. Consider why the Napoleonic system allowed him to govern France more effectively than either Louis XVI or the governments established during the Revolution.
2. Even though it limited many of the liberties promised by the Revolution, Napoleon's regime enjoyed broad support during the Consulate period. Explain the reasons for this public acceptance. Does it prove that the population had renounced the ideals of liberty and equality?
3. The question of whether Napoleon continued the Revolution or betrayed its basic principles has been debated ever since he established his regime. Analyze the arguments that can be made on both sides of this debate.

Notes

1. Leclerc, letter to Napoleon, 7 October 1802, in Paul Roussier, ed., *Lettres du Général Leclerc* (Paris: Société pour l'histoire des colonies françaises, 1937), 256.
2. Cited in J. Christopher Herold, *The Mind of Napoleon* (New York: Columbia University Press, 1955), 104.
3. Cited in Felix Markham, *Napoleon* (New York: Mentor, 1963), 95.
4. *L'Ange Gabriel*, 21 niv. VIII.

CHAPTER 8

The Napoleonic Empire, 1804–1815

LEARNING OBJECTIVES

After studying this chapter, you will be able to:

- **Explain the differences between the Napoleonic Consulate and the Empire.**
- **Describe the attitudes of major social groups toward the Empire.**
- **List the major events that led to Napoleon's defeat and the replacement of the Empire by a restored Bourbon monarchy.**

In 1804, Napoleon decided to abandon the republican facade of the Consulate. By crowning himself Emperor and making his power hereditary, he planned to make his system of one-man rule permanent. This return to the monarchical principle abandoned in 1792 meant repudiating one of the major aspects of the Revolution and renewing a link with France's historic past. Propagandists presented Napoleon as the founder of a "fourth dynasty," following the previous families of French kings, the Merovingians, the Carolingians, and the Capetians. The proclamation of the Empire was meant to demonstrate once and for all that the Revolution was over.

There was little public opposition to the proclamation of the Empire. Nevertheless, Napoleon remained uneasy about the success of his plan. His marriage to Josephine was childless. The succession law adopted along with the new constitution stated that the throne would pass to one of his brothers, but it was by no means clear that the country would accept this outcome. Nor could Napoleon be assured that the other European powers would tolerate his new system unless he convinced them that it was too powerful to be overthrown. In spite of his past successes, Napoleon felt compelled to be constantly active, reminding the French of his indispensability and the rest of Europe of his invincibility. In the early years of the Consulate, Napoleon had presented himself as a peacemaker. The constant wars during the Empire convinced even many of his own officials that he was unwilling to set any limits on his ambitions and ultimately undermined support for him. (See Document L.)

DOCUMENT L

Napoleon Reflects on His Own Career

In conversations with a faithful companion Emmanuel Las Casas during his confinement on the island of Saint Helena, Napoleon maintained that circumstances had forced him to follow authoritarian policies at home and an aggressive military policy abroad.

"When I acquired the supreme direction of affairs, it was wished that I might become a Washington.... Had I been in America, I would willingly have been a Washington, and I should have had little merit in so being; for I do not see how I could reasonably have acted otherwise. But had Washington been in France, exposed to discord within, and invasion from without, I would have defied him to have been what he was in America...For my own part, I could only have been a crowned Washington. It was only in a congress of kings, in the midst of kings yielding or subdued, that I could become so. Then and there alone, I could successfully display Washington's moderation, disinterestedness, and wisdom. I could not reasonably attain to this but by means of the universal Dictatorship. To this I aspired; can that be thought a crime?... "

(From Count Las Cases, *Life of Napoleon* [1835].)

The Resumption of War

The brief period of peace inaugurated by the treaty of Amiens with Britain in 1802 had ended even before the proclamation of the Empire. Neither side had been fully satisfied with the 1802 treaty: Napoleon still considered British sea power a threat, and the British were unwilling to accept France's domination of the Continent and the loss of their European markets. The British furnished Napoleon a pretext for breaking off relations by refusing to evacuate the island of Malta, as the treaty required, and hostilities recommenced in May 1803. Napoleon assembled an army along the Channel coast and trained it to a high pitch of readiness. Cartoonists imagined French soldiers crossing the Channel by balloon, but Britain's naval supremacy foiled any hopes of a seaborne invasion.

The resumption of the war helped convince Napoleon to proclaim himself Emperor. After the collapse of the peace of Amiens, French royalist émigrés, backed by the British, had launched a conspiracy to assassinate Napoleon. A double agent betrayed the plan to the French police, and the conspirators were arrested, but Napoleon decided that his life would remain in danger as long as it appeared that his death would bring the end of his regime. By making his rule hereditary, he hoped to convince opponents that his system would outlive him. Acting in the spirit of the Corsican tradition of vendetta in which he had been brought up, Napoleon also made a retaliatory strike against the Bourbon family. French troops invaded neutral Baden to capture the Duke d'Enghien, a Bourbon prince who Napoleon thought was implicated in plots against him. The Duke was tried in secret and executed. The execution deterred royalist plots against Napoleon's life, but it had an unfavorable effect on French public opinion. One of Napoleon's ministers supposedly remarked "it is worse than a crime, it's a blunder."

The elaborate coronation ceremony held on 2 December 1804 was carefully staged to emphasize Napoleon's glory and power. After lengthy negotiations, Pope

NAPOLEON AND HIS SOLDIERS

Napoleonic propaganda emphasized the Emperor's close bond with his men. In this illustration, ordinary soldiers act unsurprised to see their commander at their campfire.

Pius VII agreed to come from Rome, although Napoleon decided to crown himself rather than to let it appear that he owed his title to the Church. Elderly courtiers who remembered the rules of etiquette from Versailles were sought out to advise the dignitaries of the new regime, many of them originally from humble backgrounds, on proper ceremonial behavior. Although Napoleon intended the coronation to serve the serious political purpose of consolidating his reign once and for all, he was conscious of the theatrical element in the show he was arranging. "If only our father could see us now," he whispered to his brother Joseph.[1] And he remained keenly aware that, in the absence of any traditional claim to the throne, he had to keep French society under firm control and foreign enemies at bay to stay in power.

From Ulm to Tilsit

At the moment of his coronation, Napoleon's only active military foe was Britain. Britain's ability to defeat France depended on finding allies on the Continent to challenge Napoleon's land forces. The obvious candidates were Austria, which had lost both territory and prestige in its previous campaigns against France, and Russia, which had never accepted France's revolutionary conquests. British subsidies helped draw them back into the fight in August 1805, the start of a renewed round of war on the Continent that lasted until 1807. As soon as he learned of the Austro-Russian declaration of war, Napoleon marched the forces he had been training for a possible invasion of England toward the Danube. The army of 1805–1807, built around a core of soldiers with ten years of experience and commanded by battle-tested officers, was the most effective Napoleon would ever assemble, allowing him to execute complicated maneuvers on the battlefield with devastating effect.

On 20 October 1805, Napoleon's troops encircled the main Austrian army at Ulm in southern Germany and forced its surrender. A day later, off the coast of Spain, the British won the battle of Trafalgar, capturing twenty ships without losing any of their own and ending the last of the many costly efforts France had made to challenge their control of the seas. This naval defeat did not affect the land campaign, however. Six weeks later, at Austerlitz, close to Vienna, Napoleon won perhaps his most celebrated battle, completely crushing the Austrian and Russian forces. The Austrians hastened to make peace, ceding even more territory to France and its satellite states. The following year, Prussia, which had remained neutral during the 1805 campaign, unexpectedly joined Russia in the fight against Napoleon. The Emperor moved his forces into central Germany, and at the battles of Jena and Auerstädt, the French annihilated the famous Prussian army. Napoleon occupied Berlin. The Russians continued the war in 1807, as Napoleon advanced into Poland. A bloody battle at Eylau, in February 1807, was inconclusive, but in June 1807, Napoleon inflicted heavy casualties on the Russian forces at the battle of Friedland. Russia, too, sued for peace.

Napoleon met the young Russian emperor Alexander I personally at Tilsit, in Poland, to conclude a settlement to end the round of fighting that had begun two years earlier. The Peace of Tilsit of 1807 went well beyond a mere end to hostilities. The charismatic French emperor persuaded Alexander to become his partner in a grand plan by which the two powers would divide Europe and Asia into spheres of influence and work together to defeat Britain. With Russia on his side, Napoleon appeared to have achieved total control of the European Continent. He had already converted most of the "sister republics" established in the Directory period into satellite kingdoms, ruled by members of his family. Defeated Prussia and Austria had to accept Napoleon's dictates.

The Continental System

The defeat of Austria and Prussia and the peace of Tilsit gave Napoleon the opportunity to pursue a grandiose program intended to cripple his last major enemy, Britain, and to make France the dominant economic power on the Continent. Unable to directly challenge Britain's naval power, Napoleon planned a program of economic warfare that he called the Continental System. In essence, the System was an effort to block all European purchases from Britain, whose rapidly industrializing economy depended on overseas trade. Napoleon also aimed to promote the growth of French industry, which he hoped would capture the European markets Britain would lose. With his encouragement, cotton-spinning plants sprang up in Paris, which became France's largest industrial center, and in Alsace, whose location along the Rhine was favorable for export to Germany and central Europe. To replace cane sugar, previously imported from the West Indies, the government encouraged the planting of

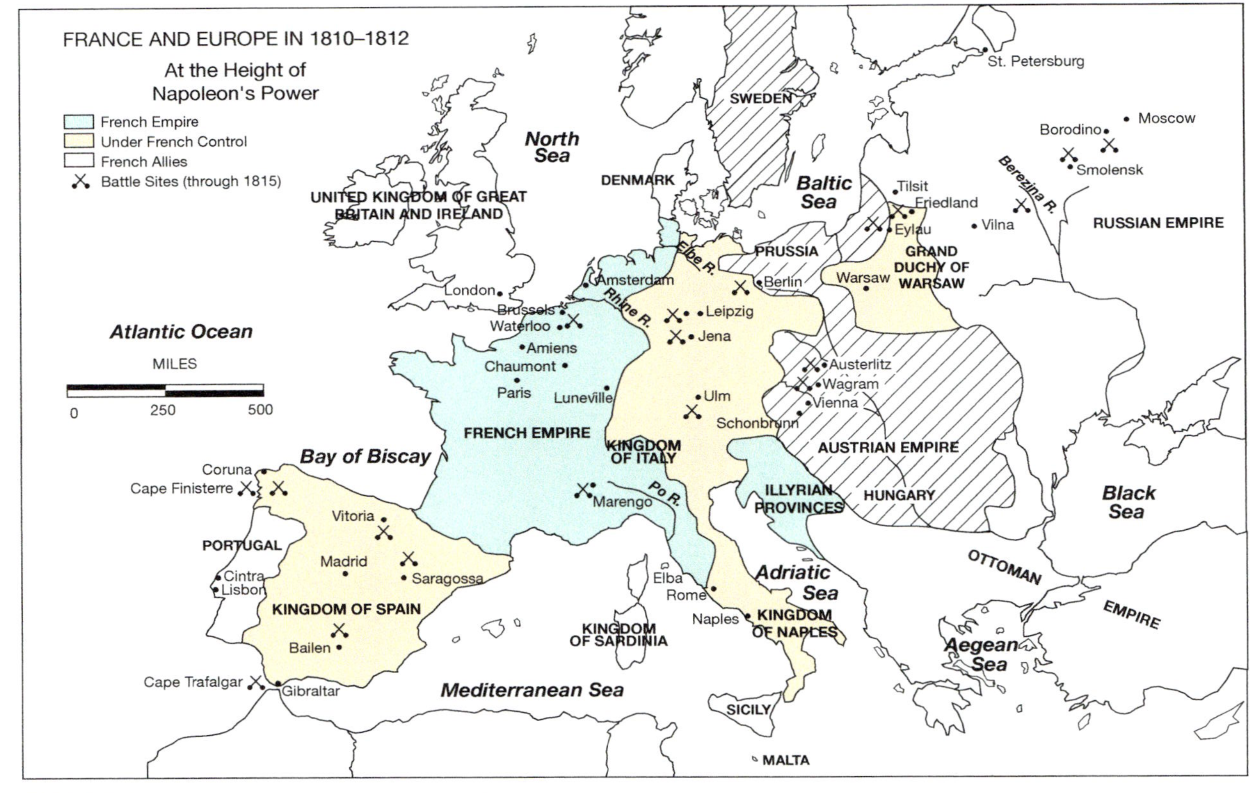

FIGURE 8.1 France and Europe under Napoleon

At the height of Napoleon's power, France's borders stretched from Rome in Italy to Hamburg in Germany. Satellite states ruled by Napoleon's relatives copied French institutions and contributed soldiers to the Imperial army. Controlling this vast area was a constant struggle for Napoleon.

sugar beets in northern France and the Belgian departments. Coal mining and iron making boomed, too, although much of the growth in this area took place in the Belgian departments that France lost after Napoleon's fall.

French manufacturers benefited from the hothouse atmosphere of the Continental System, but the port cities, hurt by the British naval blockade and the loss of France's colonies, suffered. Illegal trade with Britain flourished, undermining the boycott and driving the authorities to ever-harsher measures against local populations. To stop smuggling, Napoleon felt driven to impose tight controls on one territory after another. Spain, with its long coastline and its proximity to southern France, was one of his main concerns. In 1808, he replaced Spain's Bourbon king with his brother Joseph. This insult to Spanish national pride triggered an insurrection that tied down considerable French forces. The following year, Napoleon took over the Papal States in Italy, starting a test of wills with Pius VII that lasted until the Emperor's downfall. In 1810, Napoleon annexed northern Germany, the Netherlands, and Italy as far south as Rome directly to France, installing French prefects and French police. (See Figure 8.1)

The Empire at Home

The counterpart to Napoleon's bid for control over Europe was a steady expansion of government authority in France itself. Much of the country had welcomed the installation of an efficient system of administration during the Consulate period, when memories of the often-chaotic revolutionary decade were still fresh. But the relentless extension of government power under the Empire was less popular. Even today, the legacy of this overgrown Napoleonic bureaucracy is often cited to explain why French citizens continue to both expect and resent state involvement in almost every aspect of public life.

The increasing power of the bureaucracy went along with a further decline in the importance of the legislative branch of government. The three legislative chambers remained in existence after the declaration of the Empire in 1804, but their limited powers were even further curtailed. The Tribunate, ostensibly charged with debating laws, ceased to meet in public after 1804. In 1807, Napoleon abolished it altogether. The Imperial Senate, supposedly responsible for maintaining the constitution, became a convenient tool for changing it. Napoleon had little trouble getting the well-paid senators to pass special resolutions, called *senatus-consulta,* that avoided the necessity of calling plebiscites to approve constitutional alterations. The continued existence of the Senate and the Legislative Body served as a facade to keep the regime from looking like a straightforward revival of absolute monarchy. In 1814, however, at the moment of Napoleon's defeat, the fact that he had never entirely suppressed the legislature would give his enemies a foothold from which to challenge him.

Under the Empire, Napoleon extended centralized government control to almost every aspect of French society, including education. He abandoned the revolutionaries' ambitious plans for elementary schooling, which was left to private initiative, but the Imperial University, a bureaucratic arrangement established in 1808, gave the government a monopoly over secondary and higher education throughout the country. The secondary schools, or *lycées,* descendants of the écoles centrales established during the Directory period, were turned into military-style institutions whose students had to wear uniforms. Promising graduates served as interns attached to the Council of State, gaining experience that would qualify them for government appointments. Napoleon hoped to produce a generation of loyal state servants, but the regimented atmosphere alienated many of the brightest students and prepared them to welcome the collapse of the regime when it occurred. (See Document M.)

Napoleon used the Concordat to turn the Catholic Church into an instrument of political indoctrination. He installed his uncle, Cardinal Fesch, as head of the French Church hierarchy, ensuring its loyalty even during the years when he was locked in combat with the Pope. The Imperial Catechism, issued in 1807, taught that "to honor and serve our Emperor is to honor God himself."[2] As in the case of the schools, this heavy-handed regimentation generated a spirit of resistance. Young seminarians like the Breton Félicité de Lamennais dreamed of a Church freed from government control and loyal to the Pope. After Napoleon's fall, these Catholic "Ultramontanists," so called because they looked to a religious leader "beyond the mountains" in Italy, would transform the French Church, ending the centuries-old "Gallican" tradition that had insisted on its autonomy from Rome.

Determined to prevent the emergence of lower-class protest, Napoleon strengthened employers' powers over their workforce. An 1803 law required every worker to have a *livret,* or workbook. Workers needed their employer's signature to change jobs, and, in case of conflicts, the employer's testimony was to be accepted in court. The ban on the formation of trade unions, enacted in 1791, was reasserted in 1803. Workers did have some representation, but not an equal voice, on the *conseils de prud'hommes,* or arbitration panels, set up after 1806 to resolve conflicts between employers and employees in different trades.

In general, merchants and manufacturers managed to retain more independence from the state; the panoply of regulations characteristic of the Old Regime was not restored. But some trades considered particularly important for the maintenance of public order were tightly controlled—butchers and bakers, whose prices had the potential to incite popular protests, and printers, who were licensed in order to prevent the publication of subversive works. A state monopoly on the sale of tobacco products was set up in order to increase government revenue. Attempts to enforce the Continental Blockade added to government involvement in the economy, as customs agents raided warehouses looking for contraband goods.

The Social Bases of the Empire

The most striking feature of Napoleonic society was the increased prestige of the military, a consequence of the "war culture" fostered by the Emperor's repeated campaigns. The violence that had largely disappeared from French life after brumaire was exported abroad. Especially when they encountered guerrilla resistance, French soldiers were encouraged to respond with brutality, which incited equally extreme

DOCUMENT M

The Atmosphere of the Napoleonic Empire

In his memoirs, written in the 1850s, François Guizot, a leading nineteenth-century French liberal politician, recalled the atmosphere of the Napoleonic Empire.

"When I began my career in 1807...the intoxication of 1789 had completely dissipated. Society, absorbed in reconsolidating its foundations, was no longer interested in improving itself through its amusements. Violent spectacles had replaced its earlier desires for liberty. A lack of interest, a coldness, an isolation of feelings and of private interests, is the ordinary state of things. France, tired of illusions and bizarre excesses, eager for order and ordinary common sense, had fallen back into that morass..."

"Minds elevated above the common run and sensitive to human dignity had good reason not to like this regime, and to foresee that it would provide neither happiness nor lasting glory for France. At the time, however, it seemed so solidly supported by the general sentiment of the country, everyone was so convinced of its strength, there seemed so little possibility of a future change, that even in those exclusive circles where the spirit of opposition dominated, it seemed perfectly natural that young men should take government jobs, the only public career open to them."

(From F. Guizot, *Mémoires pour servir à l'histoire de mon temps* [Paris: Michel Lévy fréres, 1858] vol. 1, pp. 7, 13. Translation by Jeremy D. Popkin.)

responses. At home, senior officers were rewarded with honors, titles in the new Napoleonic nobility established in 1808, and landed estates in the territories France had occupied, making military careers look attractive to ambitious young men. Ceremonies like the mass award of titles in the Legion of Honor to the military in August 1804 emphasized the bond between the army and "the great man who had so often led it to victory," as a journalist wrote. Napoleon's officers supported him enthusiastically, but ordinary soldiers, separated from their homes and families for long periods, often advised younger relatives to do whatever they could to avoid being called for service. By allowing draftees to pay someone to take their place, the Napoleonic administration defused protests against conscription from wealthier families. Over time, the population learned to grudgingly accept the obligation of military service, which had caused so much resistance during the Revolution, and Napoleon knew he could count on the loyalty of his *grognards* ("grumblers") on the battlefield. By recruiting a large proportion of his troops from his non-French territories and his satellite kingdoms, Napoleon kept the human cost of his wars to France low enough to forestall protests. The French population continued to grow throughout the Napoleonic period.

While military officers made up much of the Napoleonic era's elite, Napoleon also sought to consolidate a civilian upper class that would fit his notion of a hierarchical society. Modifications to the process for selecting local government officials were intended to put power in the hands of large landowners, the "masses of granite" whom Napoleon regarded as the natural leaders of society. This elite included both members of the prerevolutionary aristocracy who had preserved or restored their holdings and the new nobility that Napoleon himself created. Members of the bourgeoisie consolidated their hold on the government posts opened up to them after 1789. State licensing of physicians, imposed in 1803, and the restoration of the bar in 1811 re-created the professional monopolies that benefitted doctors and lawyers, which had been abolished during the revolutionary period. As under the Old Regime, the bourgeoisie continued to invest much of its acquired wealth in land, imitating the behavior of the aristocracy rather than adopting a new set of values.

It has often been argued that the Napoleonic regime had a special appeal for the country's peasants, who still made up the overwhelming majority of the population. The Napoleonic land settlement guaranteed that peasants who had purchased land from Church and noble holdings during the 1790s could keep it. Prosperous peasants continued to acquire property during the Napoleonic period, as investors who had bought large estates during the Revolution sold them off piecemeal. Under Napoleon, villagers lost the freedom to choose their own local officials that the Revolution had given them, but the regime provided an efficient administrative system and a uniform set of laws that most peasants preferred to the seigneurial regime. The Napoleonic armies provided an outlet for surplus population and an opportunity for social advancement for some peasants. During this period, France became more than ever a country of small family farms, in contrast to England where large landowners were using the process of enclosure to drive less prosperous neighbors off the land. Although peasants counted on Napoleon to protect them against the loss of Church and noble lands purchased during the Revolution, they did resent Imperial taxes and the burden of military conscription, both of which increased in the last years of the regime. The urban working classes' situation in this period was less favorable. Police supervision prevented any visible agitation among the population, and former sans-culotte activists faded back into the anonymity of private life. Urban poverty was still widespread. The large numbers of prostitutes active in Paris testified to the number of poor women who remained unable to make a living in any other way. But even the sharp economic crisis of 1811 saw no repetition of the mass protests that had marked the revolutionary decade. Not until the July Revolution of 1830, fifteen years after the end of the Napoleonic era, did France's urban poor reappear as an active force in public life.

Napoleon's narrow notion about women's roles was reflected in the Civil Code's restriction of their legal rights. As part of the regime's systematic effort to regulate behavior, prostitutes were subjected to police controls and mandatory health inspections, a gendered form of discipline that remained in effect in France until after World War II. Women were not entirely banished from public life: they were encouraged to attend public ceremonies, in part because their presence ensured that more men would come, and they were often honored for their roles as wives and mothers. Napoleon discouraged women's education, writing that religious instruction was suited to "the weakness of women's brains, the mobility of their ideas, their destination in the social order," which he defined as marriage and child-rearing.[3] Except among the wealthy, however, women usually worked to contribute to family income and, in some cases, women were able to resist male authority. Catholic nurses, allowed to resume their work in hospitals under Napoleon, successfully defied his effort to make them give up their religious vows. Women even had a role in Napoleonic warfare. The laundrywomen and the *cantinières* who sold liquor and refreshments to the soldiers provided indispensable services and enjoyed a certain amount of official recognition.

Culture Under the Empire

Napoleon intended to make art and culture serve the purposes of the state. The Louvre museum, enriched with artwork confiscated from conquered territories, exemplified his ambition to make Paris the unquestioned center of European culture. The "Empire style" that characterized the period's decorative arts featured Egyptian motifs that recalled Napoleon's expedition of 1798. Napoleon intervened personally in cultural matters, even interrupting his military campaigns to send instructions settling quarrels among theater performers in Paris. The Imperial government was an active patron, commissioning numerous paintings glorifying the Emperor and his accomplishments. Jacques-Louis David, once an enthusiastic supporter of Robespierre, now put his talents in the service of the new regime, painting several famous portraits of Napoleon, including a dramatic depiction of him on horseback and a huge canvas representing the Emperor's coronation. Antoine-Jean Gros painted a Christlike Napoleon visiting plague victims during his Egyptian campaign, and J.-A.-D. Ingres, perhaps David's most famous disciple, began his long career with an elaborate portrait of the Emperor in his coronation robes. The revival of the art market after the disruptions of the revolutionary decade did allow painters to pursue other projects besides the glorification of the ruler, however. Recent art historians have noted a growing interest in scenes from exotic lands, subjects from medieval literature and history, and portraits and allegorical scenes with psychological overtones. These developments pointed toward the more fully developed romantic art that would flourish after Napoleon's fall.

Napoleon planned to make Paris a monument to his own glory and that of the army. A long, straight boulevard, the rue de Rivoli, was to traverse the city, and Roman-style monuments, including a column surmounted with a statue of the Emperor in the Place Vendôme and two Arches of Triumph, were to celebrate his military victories. Only the smaller of these, the Arch of the Carousel, located between the Louvre and the Tuileries gardens, was completed during his reign. The great Arch of Triumph at the Etoile, still one of Paris's best-known monuments, was finally finished in the mid-nineteenth century, serving as a monument to the French armies rather than to Napoleon alone.

The imperial period was less favorable for French authors. Playwrights learned that any reference to politics or history could be interpreted as criticism of the regime; with the theater stifled by censorship, audiences turned to the less controversial entertainments of the boulevard theaters, which featured acrobats and animal shows. Madame de Staël, alienated from Napoleon during the Consulate period, spent most of the Empire in exile. Her book *On Germany*, published in 1810, contrasted the independent spirit of the early romantic philosophers and poets in Germany with the repressive atmosphere in France. The Catholic Chateaubriand also fell out of favor for comparing Napoleon to the Roman emperor Nero. The authorities found ingenious ways to muffle potential criticism, such as forcing the editors of the pro-Catholic *Mercure de France* and the rationalist Idéologue journal *La Décade philosophique* to merge their two publications. Not surprisingly, writers and intellectuals of almost every persuasion welcomed the Empire's downfall in 1814.

The Decline of the Empire

Even at the height of Napoleon's reign, from 1807 to 1810, his hold on Europe was never secure. Napoleon's own officials often realized that the Empire was extending itself too far; Talleyrand, the foreign minister, secretly encouraged other governments to resist French expansion. In some occupied territories, the French were able to persuade local elites to cooperate with them, but in other areas, they encountered violent opposition. The "Spanish ulcer," the guerrilla war against French domination that had begun in 1808, became as brutal as the Vendée rebellion and the conflict in Haiti. Spain swallowed up increasing numbers of French troops and provided an opening for the British, who landed an expeditionary force under General Wellington in Portugal in 1809. With French troops tied up in Spain, Austria decided to make a new bid to shake off French domination in 1809. Napoleon defeated the Austrians at Wagram, another of his most famous battles, but he himself was well aware of how thin his forces had been stretched. He no longer had the luxury of commanding a thoroughly trained veteran army, as he had in 1805. His forces now included a much larger proportion of hastily recruited non-French soldiers, and he had to simplify his battle tactics and put increasing reliance on his elite striking force, the Imperial Guard. Napoleon also faced an open conflict with Pope Pius VII, who refused to integrate his territories into the Continental System and excommunicated the Emperor when he seized them by force. An exasperated Napoleon had the Pope put under house arrest in a small Italian town and later brought him to France. The Pope retaliated by refusing to consecrate bishops nominated to fill vacancies in France, leading Napoleon to try to force the French clergy to agree that he could install bishops without Papal approval after a six-month delay. This proposal threatened to revive the conflict between the state and the Church that had marked the 1790s, but before a complete rupture occurred, military defeats forced Napoleon to turn his attention elsewhere.

Napoleon tried to counter these mounting difficulties by strengthening his ties with other European rulers. In 1810, he divorced the childless Josephine and married an Austrian princess, Marie-Louise, who bore him a son in 1812, thus raising hopes for the permanence of the dynasty. This rapprochement with Austria did not solve his mounting problems, however. The Continental System had begun to unravel; Napoleon himself connived at violations of it, selling licenses for trade with Britain as a means of raising money. In December 1810, Russia abruptly withdrew from the System and resumed trade with Britain, convincing Napoleon that Alexander intended to turn against him. To distract the British, Napoleon tried to push the United States into a conflict with them. War between the two countries did break out in 1812, but by this time, Napoleon had alienated even longtime Francophiles like Thomas Jefferson. "His domineering temper deafens him...to the dictates of interest, of honor and of morality," Jefferson wrote to the American minister in Paris.[4] In

France itself, the year 1810 was marked by the beginning of a sharp economic crisis that persisted into 1811. French manufacturing slumped, and factory owners joined the merchants of the port cities in blaming the regime for their troubles.

The Invasion of Russia

Napoleon responded to his mounting difficulties with his tried-and-true formula: a daring military campaign to convince his foes of his invincibility. But this time his gamble—an invasion of Russia to force it back into the Continental System—failed. With an army of over half a million men, most of them recruited from territories outside France, he crossed the Russian border in June 1812. This huge force proved too cumbersome to employ the tactics of rapid movement and maneuverability that had brought Napoleon success in previous campaigns. The outnumbered Russians retreated, avoiding a decisive engagement, with the result that Napoleon was drawn further and further from his supply bases. At Borodino, near Moscow, the two armies fought the bloodiest battle of the period, losing a combined 70,000 men in one day, but the Russians then slipped away again, leaving Napoleon to occupy their capital without opposition.

The conquest of Moscow was a hollow victory. The Russian forces remained intact, and Alexander refused to negotiate. Most of the city burned down in a fire shortly after the French moved in, leaving the army without supplies or shelter. Napoleon finally had to begin a retreat as the harsh Russian winter set in. Cold, hunger, and Russian harassment decimated his troops; less than one-tenth of the men who had set off for Moscow returned. When news of the defeat reached Paris, conspirators spread the rumor that Napoleon himself had been killed. In the hours of confusion caused by the coup attempt, Napoleon's top officials failed to follow plans to declare his infant son Emperor, revealing how shaky the regime's support had become. Napoleon had to hurry back to France to restore order.

Even after the defeat in Russia, Napoleon still thought that his own military genius and the potential divisions among his foes would allow him to reverse the situation. In 1813, he pulled together a new army, made up mostly of raw recruits and men previously rejected as unfit. This greatly increased demand for conscripts revived unhappiness with the regime at home. Abroad, one government after another, led by Prussia and then Austria, sensed that the tide had turned and joined the coalition against him. In October 1813, the combined allied forces defeated him at the battle of Leipzig, and Napoleon had to retreat across the Rhine; meanwhile, British and Spanish forces under the Duke of Wellington advanced toward the Pyrenees. As the enemy forces penetrated into France in the winter of 1814, Napoleon fought a skillful rearguard campaign, but he was hopelessly outnumbered. The French population, whose patriotism had enabled the revolutionary armies to fight off invaders in 1792 and 1793, refused to heed Napoleon's summons to rise to the nation's defense. For too long, he had smothered all real participation in public affairs; ordinary citizens now responded by leaving him to his fate. At the end of March 1814, allied forces reached Paris.

Although military defeat was now certain, it was not clear that the Napoleonic regime would also fall. Royalist conspirators' efforts to set off demonstrations in favor of a Bourbon restoration enjoyed success in some regions, particularly the southwest, but the victorious allies were not convinced that a government hostile to the Revolution could assure stability without becoming totally dependent on them for support. They were therefore receptive to overtures from Napoleon's former foreign minister Talleyrand, who headed the Imperial Senate that Napoleon had never abolished. Talleyrand and his followers were prepared to reinstate the Bourbons, but on their own terms: Louis XVI's long-exiled brother would be put on the throne as king, but he would have to accept a written constitution limiting his power and maintaining the principal features of the "Napoleonic settlement." Those who had obtained high governmental positions under Napoleon would keep them, and purchasers of Church and émigré property would not be disturbed. The opportunistic Talleyrand, who had served every successive French government since the Old Regime, and the police minister Fouché, a former Convention deputy who had voted for the execution of Louis XVI, retained their offices. Napoleon, warned by his generals that the army would not continue the fight, abdicated his throne on 6 April 1814. Twenty-five years of revolutionary upheaval and Napoleonic rule had brought France back to a system of constitutional monarchy similar to what many reformers had hoped for in the spring of 1789.

The Hundred Days

The restoration of the Bourbons in 1814 was meant to mark the end of the revolutionary and Napoleonic era, but Napoleon was still to add an unexpected chapter to his epic story. The victorious allies exiled him to the small island of Elba off the coast of Italy. From this observation post, he kept close watch on events in France. The new king, Louis XVIII, soon encountered major difficulties in consolidating his regime. His return was followed by an influx of die-hard émigrés who had remained in exile throughout the Napoleonic period. They agitated for the return of their confiscated estates and for the restoration of the prerevolutionary system of privileges. The appointment of émigré military officers who had fought against France to posts in the French army outraged patriotic sentiment, especially since the end of the war had brought massive layoffs at all ranks. The fact that the new Restoration monarchy was propped up by foreign occupying forces made it easy to turn French nationalist sentiment against it.

Emboldened by reports of unrest in France, Napoleon took a dramatic gamble. On 1 March 1815, having slipped past British patrol ships, he landed on the Mediterranean coast. Accompanied by a small band of loyal troops, he began to march north to Paris. Military units sent to arrest him, composed mostly of veterans of his earlier campaigns, went over to his side as he advanced. On 19 March, Louis XVIII fled Paris, and Napoleon entered the capital the following day, inaugurating the "Hundred Days" of his last bid for power.

The Restoration government's unpopular gestures in favor of nobles and émigrés gave Napoleon a broader base of support than in 1814; a spontaneous movement of volunteers, the *fédérés,* rallied to him and intimidated potential opponents. Napoleon was reluctant to encourage a real resurgence of popular radicalism, however. He made a greater effort to reach out to liberals and members of the middle classes.

Benjamin Constant, a longtime critic of the Empire's authoritarianism, drafted an "Additional Act" to the Imperial Constitution, meant to protect individual rights and constitutional government. Napoleon even refrained from punishing the high officials who had betrayed him in 1814. Fouché, the police minister, remained in office, although Napoleon had ample reason to suspect his loyalty. But Napoleon remained uneasily aware that many areas of the country, such as the west, where royalist sentiment had always been strong, still opposed him.

Napoleon's only chance of consolidating his position was to force the other European powers to accept his return. After fifteen years of almost continual warfare, other governments had no faith in Napoleon's statements about his peaceful intentions. The allied coalition renewed the war, and Napoleon once again had to risk his regime's fate on the battlefield. Reassembling as much of his Grand Army as he could, Napoleon marched into Belgium, hoping to defeat the British and Prussians separately before the Austrians and Russians could join them. He caught the British at the village of Waterloo, near Brussels, but this time, luck was not with him. Many of his best generals had betrayed him in 1814 or no longer showed the fighting spirit of earlier years. The experienced British veterans under the command of the Duke of Wellington, the architect of France's defeat in Spain, held off even Napoleon's feared Imperial Guard. Napoleon retreated to Paris, but he immediately realized that there was no chance of preserving his power. He surrendered to the British, who exiled him to the remote South Atlantic island of Saint Helena for the six remaining years of his life. Louis XVIII followed the allied troops back to his capital. His second restoration, in July 1815, finally put an end to the long drama of the revolutionary and Napoleonic period.

Critical Thinking Questions

1. In 1804, Napoleon established a hereditary Empire in place of the earlier Consulate. Describe the differences between these two regimes. Did the creation of the Empire amount to a complete break with the heritage of the Revolution?
2. The Napoleonic regime attempted to appeal to all major groups of the population. How successful was it in gaining real support from them? Explain which groups most enthusiastically supported Napoleon, and which were most difficult for him to win over.
3. By 1810, Napoleon had conquered almost all of Continental Europe, but by 1814, he was forced to give up power, and his effort to regain it in 1815 was quickly defeated. Describe how Napoleon's own actions led to his defeat. Could he have avoided the overthrow of his regime?

Notes

1. Cited in Felix Markham, *Napoleon* (New York: Mentor, 1963), 113.
2. Cited in Rafe Blaufard, *Napoleon: Symbol for an Age* (Boston: Bedford, 2008), 96.
3. Cited in J. Christopher Herold, *The Mind of Napoleon* (New York: Columbia University Press, 1955), 18.
4. Cited in James Woodness, *A Yankee's Odyssey: The Life of Joel Barlow* (Philadelphia: Lippincott, 1958), 277.

CHAPTER 9

The Revolutionary Heritage

LEARNING OBJECTIVES

After studying this chapter, you will be able to:

- **List the enduring changes brought about by the Revolution.**
- **Retrace the major phases of historical writing about the Revolution.**
- **Explain why historians continue to disagree about the significance of the Revolution.**

Superficially, Napoleon's downfall appeared to bring France back to the point where the Revolution had started. The Bourbon dynasty was restored and, after spending twenty-five years in exile, Louis XVI's brother was proclaimed as Louis XVIII. However, the Revolution had caused deep and permanent changes in French society. As Alfred de Musset, one of the generation of French writers who grew up in the years immediately following Napoleon's fall, wrote, "the powers divine and human were in fact reestablished, but belief in them no longer existed."[1] Louis XVIII largely accepted this situation. He made little effort to reinstate the privileges of the nobility or the Church, and he accepted the necessity of governing according to a written constitution that provided for a legislative assembly, one of whose chambers was elected.

Louis XVIII's acceptance of many of the Revolution's key reforms enabled him to reign peacefully until his death in 1824. He was succeeded by his less flexible brother, Charles X, whose intransigent policies provoked a new revolution in 1830 that replaced the Restoration with a new constitutional monarchy headed by his cousin, Louis-Philippe d'Orléans. During the next half century, France repeated in slow motion the revolutionary cycle that had begun in 1789. The Orleanist regime set up in 1830 was overthrown in another revolution in 1848 and replaced with by the democratic Second Republic, which was in turn overthrown by Napoleon Bonaparte's nephew in 1851. Taking the title of Napoleon III, he re-established the Empire, which lasted until France's calamitous defeat by Germany in 1870–1871. That defeat opened the possibility of a return to monarchy, but it soon became clear that the population would accept only a regime based on the democratic and republican principles of the revolutionary era. The passage of a constitution establishing France's Third Republic in 1875 closed the long era of political instability that had started in 1789.

The Postrevolutionary Settlement

France's political instability in the nineteenth century masked the fact that many of the fundamental changes made during the Revolution were never seriously challenged after 1789. The principles of liberty and equality had sunk deep roots by 1815. The result was a society made up of independent male citizens, governed by a greatly strengthened centralized state. Although the various nineteenth-century regimes often curtailed the political freedoms promised in 1789, the belief that French citizens nevertheless had an equal right to do "all that is not forbidden by the law," as the original Declaration of Rights had stated, survived. Incorporated in the provisions of the Napoleonic Code, which remained the law of the land, this individualistic outlook barred any return to the corporatist society of the Old Regime, with its numerous restrictions on economic enterprise. The revolutionary and Napoleonic era had also defined the legal and political position of women. Denied political rights by the revolutionary legislators and subordinated to their fathers and husbands by the Napoleonic Code, French women would have a long struggle to gain equal status with men. Within the home, however, the importance of their role in shaping children's character was increasingly recognized.

The revolutionary heritage of egalitarianism prevented any reestablishment of hereditary social status. Noble titles still commanded social prestige, but they no longer carried any legal privileges or tax exemptions. Government jobs—more numerous than ever as a result of the growth of the administration during the revolutionary era—were now open to men from all social classes. As France gradually entered the industrial era after 1815, prosperous bourgeois manufacturers, bankers, and professionals supplanted landowners as the country's wealthy elite. This bourgeois class benefited from the Revolution's protection of property rights, but so did much of the peasantry. The parceling out of the former church holdings and of many noble estates created a rural democracy of small landowners, freed from the collective restrictions that had governed village life before 1789. Together, the strengthened bourgeoisie and the landholding peasantry that emerged from the revolutionary era proved a formidable obstacle both to the return of old privileged groups and to the claims of new ones, such as the propertyless industrial proletariat that developed in the nineteenth century.

Property rights were not the only evidence of the Revolution's extension of individual freedom. The Revolution's secularization of French society also proved permanent. Not only did Protestants and Jews now have the same rights as Catholics, but much of the population also exercised its right not to practice any religion. Although freedom for the newspaper press remained restricted for much of the nineteenth century, censorship of books was not reinstated: access to a variety of ideas and opinions came to be regarded as a fundamental right.

The revolutionaries of 1789 had proclaimed that individual rights could be protected only by a written constitution and a representative government. These basic principles have been incorporated in all of the country's postrevolutionary regimes, with the exception of the Vichy government established during the German occupation of 1940–1944. Written constitutions have changed frequently since 1815, and elections have not always given voters a true chance to express their wishes, but France has always had some kind of elected assembly with the power to make laws and approve government expenditures. The revolutionary principle of national sovereignty has thus come to be a fundamental feature of the country's political culture.

State and Nation

Like the changes it had made in individual rights, the Revolution's reshaping of France's governmental structure proved to be permanent. The elimination of the parlements, the provinces, and the multitude of local privileges carried out on the night of 4 August 1789 had cleared the way for the creation of an efficient central administration and a national court system, which no subsequent French regime has tried to change. The government kept the functions, such as registering births, marriages, and deaths, that it had taken over from the Church after 1789. The equal-sized *départements* which replaced the old provinces also endured. All these reforms accentuated the centralization of power in the capital, already evident before 1789 but greatly increased by the Revolution and Napoleon.

The centralized postrevolutionary government ruled over a unified nation. As the legislators of 1789 had intended, the same laws now governed the entire country. The tolls and customs duties that had divided the country economically no longer existed, and all parts of the country now paid the same taxes. Although it took much of the nineteenth century to establish a national system of elementary schools, the central government now had firm control of secondary and higher education. Schooling, the necessity of understanding laws and regulations issued in Paris, and the habit of following events through the newspapers all favored the spread of a standardized French language at the expense of regional dialects.

Postrevolutionary France still retained some connections with the world of the Old Regime. Peasants were still a majority of the population throughout the nineteenth century, and farming methods changed only slowly. Regional loyalties remained in people's minds, even though the historic provinces had been abolished. But the shared experience of the Revolution and the Napoleonic wars gave the country a new set of historical memories that overshadowed what had come before. Throughout the nineteenth century and into the twentieth, the basic issues that divided the French people usually traced their origins to the struggles of the revolutionary period. In 1989, the attempt to organize a national commemoration of the events that had created modern France revived old controversies. François Mitterrand, France's president at the time, proudly reminded his fellow citizens that the Revolution had been "a decisive part of France in the evolution of the world and of human society," even though he did acknowledge the "deviations, oppressions, and later derelictions" that had marred its record.[2]

The Revolution's Impact in the World

Just as it has continued to affect France for over two centuries, the French Revolution has had a lasting impact in other parts of the world. The French Revolution has inspired many imitators. The ideals of individual rights, constitutional government, and national sovereignty articulated in 1789 have inspired movements for freedom and democracy throughout the world, from the revolts against Spanish rule in South America at the beginning of the 1800s to the Russian Revolution of 1917 and the movements of the "Arab Spring" in 2011. The Universal Declaration of Human Rights, adopted by the United Nations in 1948 as a statement of the principles to which all countries should adhere, owes much of its inspiration to the Declaration of the Rights of Man and Citizen.

At the same time, however, the French Revolution has also shown how easily revolutionary movements can result in violence and dictatorship. Violence accompanied every major stage of the Revolution, underlining the difficulty of making radical, social, and political changes without raising passions to dangerous levels. In its efforts to defend itself against real and imagined foes, the French Revolution provided the first model of the totalitarian state, silencing all opposition and sometimes aspiring to efface all diversity in the name of the public good. The revolutionary government of the Terror also showed how such a regime could mobilize the entire force of a large country for military purposes. The French Revolution inaugurated the age of total warfare, foreshadowing the horrendous conflicts of the twentieth century. The rise of Napoleon showed that the conflicts generated by revolutionary upheaval could drive a population to accept dictatorial rule as the only way to achieve stability.

The legacy of the French Revolution is thus a complex one. It provokes continuing controversy because it raises the most fundamental issues about how societies should be structured. In our own age, when contacts between different cultures have become so much more extensive, the Revolution's liberal and democratic ideals have renewed importance. Broadened to cover all of the world's citizens, they can be seen as offering a set of principles on the basis of which the ancient Biblical promise of a world in which all nations can live together in harmony might be realized.

The French Revolution as History

The experience of the French Revolution helped form the modern historical consciousness. Those who lived through it learned that a long-established society could be shattered and remade almost overnight. They also learned that events could escape the control of those who set them in motion and lead to outcomes that contradicted their original goals. Throughout Europe, the French Revolution was a tremendous stimulus to the study of history—not just the history of the French Revolution but also the study of the general mechanisms that shape historical events. The ways in which historians interpret the French Revolution often serve as models for the understanding of other great historical occurrences.

The first important histories of the French Revolution were strongly affected by the political currents of nineteenth-century French life. During the Restoration, when the official policy of the French government was to repress all memory of the

Revolution, the liberal historian Adolphe Thiers's *History of the French Revolution* was a manifesto in favor of the ideals of 1789. Thiers celebrated the reformist leaders of the National Assembly and tried to exculpate them of responsibility for the radicalism and violence of the Reign of Terror. Under the July Monarchy, Jules Michelet produced a populist narrative of the Revolution, insisting on the importance of the role of the national spirit embodied in the common people. His work, strongly colored by the romantic spirit of the times, can be seen as the first attempt to capture the experience of the Revolution "from the bottom up."

Historians writing after the failure of the Revolution of 1848 tended to be more critical of the 1789 movement. Alexis de Tocqueville's masterpiece *The Old Regime and the Revolution,* published in 1856, was the first serious attempt to analyze and explain the revolutionary process, rather than simply to narrate its major events and judge its major actors. Without realizing it, Tocqueville maintained, the revolutionaries were continuing the work of the Bourbon monarchy, creating a centralized, bureaucratic government and destroying the organic connections between citizens of different classes. As a result, he concluded, they had furthered equality but undermined the preconditions for the liberty that they thought they were establishing. Tocqueville's insistence on the continuities between the Old Regime and the revolutionary era and his argument that what the revolutionaries intended was quite different from what they achieved were fundamental contributions to the historical understanding of 1789.

The Jacobin Historical Synthesis

Modern scientific scholarship on the French Revolution began with the appointment of Alphonse Aulard to the first academic chair of revolutionary history in the early 1880s. Aulard stressed the importance of detailed and thorough archival research, setting standards that still guide serious historical inquiry in the field today. He edited publications of primary source materials that are still of value and used his mastery of the archives to clarify many important episodes of revolutionary politics.

Aulard was also the founding figure in what has come to be called the classic, or Jacobin, interpretation of the Revolution. For Aulard, a firm supporter of the Third Republic, the heroes of the Revolution were the democratic republicans of the 1790s, who had ensured the victory of the ideals articulated by the liberal revolutionaries of 1789. In contrast to Tocqueville, Aulard stressed the differences between the Old Regime and the Revolution rather than the continuities between them. He blamed the Terror and the Revolution's difficulties on the necessity of combating counterrevolutionary forces at home and their foreign allies. In his view, Georges Danton, the energetic leader who had rallied the country in 1792 and 1793, personified the spirit of the democratic and republican revolution.

By the beginning of the twentieth century, the socialist doctrines of Karl Marx had come to have considerable influence in French politics and intellectual life. The French socialist leader Jean Jaurès inspired the publication of a *Socialist History of the French Revolution* (1901–1904), which put new emphasis on the social and economic aspects of the movement. Earlier liberal and republican historians, including Aulard, had acknowledged the leading role of the bourgeois class in the

Revolution. The socialist analysis explained this role in terms of the bourgeoisie's interest in overthrowing the old aristocracy and in creating the conditions for an expanding capitalist economy.

Between them, Aulard and Jaurès provided a basic framework that governed most scholarly analysis of the French Revolution until the 1960s. Historians imbued with this tradition see the Revolution as a sharp break with the Old Regime that preceded it and as a necessary and an inevitable step toward modern secular democracy. They generally argue that "the Revolution is a bloc," in the words of the French republican politician Georges Clemenceau. By this, they mean that the success of the liberal reforms enacted by the National Assembly in 1789 was only assured thanks to the radical measures taken by the Jacobins after 1792. In this interpretation, the Terror is seen as a necessary aspect of the revolutionary process, essential to defeating the hostile forces at home and abroad that would otherwise have restored the Old Regime.

Many twentieth-century historians, sympathetic to the plight of the proletariat, claimed that the "bourgeois" revolution of 1789 provided a model for a future proletarian revolution that would finally ensure liberty and equality for all classes of the population. Many—but by no means all—historians of the French Revolution came to see the Bolshevik Revolution of 1917 in Russia as a confirmation of the Marxist interpretation of history. This view in turn influenced their understanding of 1789, leading them to emphasize the theme of class struggle and to highlight those aspects of the French experience that anticipated what had happened in Russia.

The most prominent historians who contributed to this classical interpretation of the French Revolution after Aulard were the three French scholars Albert Mathiez, Georges Lefebvre, and Albert Soboul. Each occupied the Sorbonne's chair of the history of the French Revolution for many years, training numerous students and influencing research on the Revolution not only in France but in other countries as well. Each also broadened the scope of the classical interpretation in important ways. Albert Mathiez denounced Aulard's hero, Danton, as a corrupt demagogue. In his view, only Robespierre had understood the necessity of uniting the bourgeoisie and the common people and of taking the tough measures that guaranteed the survival of the Revolution's achievements. Mathiez also contributed to a better understanding of the way in which economic conditions affected the course of the Revolution. He demonstrated the close correlation between high bread prices and lower-class unrest in Paris throughout the 1790s. Mathiez's work helped make sense of the radical Montagnard movement, which, he claimed, under pressure from the lower classes, had begun to propose measures that went beyond bourgeois democracy and foreshadowed the development of socialism.

Georges Lefebvre is remembered above all for elucidating the vital role of the peasants in the Revolution. His meticulous regional study of the department of the Nord showed that peasant populations were not an inarticulate mass, simply reacting to decrees from Paris. Peasants had concerns of their own, different from those of the bourgeois deputies in the Paris assemblies. Lefebvre's study *The Great Fear of 1789* was a pioneering analysis of collective mentalities, and his clear and readable synthesis *The Coming of the French Revolution,* published in 1939, introduced several generations of French and American students to revolutionary history. Lefebvre offered a sophisticated Marxist analysis that explained the course of the Revolution in terms of changing alliances between four social groups: the aristocracy, whose resistance to necessary reforms set the Revolution in motion; the bourgeoisie, which provided leadership and a revolutionary program; the peasantry, whose uprising in 1789 assured the Revolution's success; and the urban lower classes, whose pressure drove the bourgeois leadership to take the measures necessary to protect the Revolution after 1792.

Lefebvre's student Albert Soboul turned his attention to the sans-culottes, the urban militants who played such an important role in the Revolution's radical phase. He gave new precision to historians' picture of this group, showing that they were not the poorest members of the Paris population but rather shopkeepers, skilled artisans, and small businessmen, generally literate and capable of forming their own political ideas, independent of bourgeois leaders. While Soboul continued the Jacobin historical tradition in France, several English-speaking historians trained by Lefebvre introduced the social-historical approach to the subject to the English-speaking world. George Rudé's *The Crowd in the French Revolution* showed that urban revolutionary violence was neither random nor purposeless. The crowd was made up of the better-off, more aware members of the urban lower classes, and its actions expressed a definite political agenda. Richard Cobb's *The People's Armies* added to historians' understanding of the role of the sans-culottes during the Terror. In many subsequent books and articles, Cobb broadened the study of ordinary people's experiences during the Revolution. Over time, however, he broke away from the Marxist emphasis on the importance of class conflicts, arguing that individual experience during the Revolution was too diverse to be understood in such categories.

The Revisionist Critique

By the early 1960s, academic historians throughout the world seemed in agreement on the basic issues involved in understanding the French Revolution. Only a few questioned the idea that 1789 had been above all an expression of social conflict stemming from the bourgeoisie's dissatisfaction with the Old Regime and the lower classes' resentment of their lot. To be sure, there were some dissenters. In an essay entitled "The Myth of the French Revolution," an English historian, Alfred Cobban, charged that Marxist historians such as Lefebvre and Soboul had misread their own evidence. The bourgeois participants in 1789, Cobban maintained, were not economically progressive merchants and manufacturers trying to create a capitalist order, but primarily owners of royal offices, irate because the Old Regime's incompetence was undermining their hard-won positions. An American historian, G. H. Taylor, challenged the notion of a conflict between a "feudal" aristocracy and a "capitalist" bourgeoisie by showing that both groups tended to invest their wealth in similar ways, above all by acquiring landed estates.

In the 1970s, these scattered calls for a revision of the standard approach to the French Revolution were given new polemical vigor by a French scholar, François Furet. In essays later published in English under the title *Interpreting the French Revolution* (1981), Furet denounced what he called the "catechism" of historical orthodoxy that had come to dominate the field. Critical of Marxism, Furet questioned whether a model based on social classes corresponded to the reality of eighteenth-century life. He pointed out that the revolutionary decade retarded the growth of capitalism, rather than promoting it. He also denied that pressure from counterrevolutionary forces explained the Revolution's path from liberal reforms to bloody dictatorship. In Furet's view, the politics of the Revolution was not a reflection of underlying class conflict. It was rather a violent competition of "discourses," as rival groups sought to manipulate strategic slogans to their advantage. Furthermore, Furet questioned whether the Revolution had contributed to the development of liberal institutions. Like Tocqueville, whom he greatly admired, Furet suggested that the Revolution had been unable to break away from the authoritarian framework of the French past and that it did more to set back the cause of freedom than to advance it. Going beyond Furet, some French historians, particularly those who studied the Vendée rebellion, went so far as to label the Terror an instance of genocide.

Postrevisionist Studies of the Revolution

Furet's outspoken essay, the best summation of what came to be known as the "revisionist" critique of the Jacobin historiographical tradition, galvanized new interest in the Revolution's history throughout the late 1970s and the 1980s. Caught up in the general crisis of the Marxist tradition, the defenders of what was now stigmatized as the "orthodox" view of the Revolution were thrown on the defensive. By 1980, a leading English historian, William Doyle, began his reconsideration of *The Origins of the French Revolution* by announcing that the traditional historical framework for the subject had "collapsed." As Doyle acknowledged, however, there was no consensus on how it should be replaced. Doyle himself was one of a number of historians who argued for a return to the primacy of political history. Doyle's own *Oxford History of the French Revolution* (2nd ed., 2003) offers a detailed narrative along these lines.

Historians who questioned whether the French Revolution was best defined as a sudden shift from a feudal and aristocratic order to a capitalist and bourgeois epoch implicitly raised the question of how much of a break with the past the events of 1789–1815 actually represented. Most recent researchers have concluded that the Revolution did not mark a radical break in France's economic development. The fundamental transition to economic modernity that we label "the industrial revolution" did not arrive in France until the 1830s and 1840s. Although the Revolution abolished the political privileges of the nobility, French life remained dominated until the middle of the nineteenth century by an elite of "notables" whose wealth was still mainly in the form of agricultural land. Among peasants and workers, old patterns of collective protest persisted until at least the 1830s, suggesting that the Revolution had not caused a fundamental change in mentalities. If there was a distinct period when France changed rapidly from a "traditional" society to a "modern" one, many recent historians have suggested that it should be dated around the middle of the nineteenth century.

Most historians who specialize in the French Revolution, however, have continued to argue that it did represent a fundamental crisis in France's history. They have reacted to the evidence that the Revolution did not bring about massive changes in economic or social structures by turning in new directions for inspiration, drawing on insights from anthropology and linguistics to demonstrate that 1789 created a new culture and new patterns of thought and behavior. Pioneering examples of what came to be labeled "the new cultural history" during the 1980s included Mona Ozouf's study of *Festivals and the French Revolution* (1979), Lynn Hunt's *Politics, Culture, and Class in the French Revolution* (1984), and Timothy Tackett's *Religion, Revolution, and Regional Culture in Eighteenth-Century France* (1986). All three emphasized the importance of new rituals, new symbols, and new patterns of social behavior in defining the Revolution, as opposed to stressing the redistribution of property or the actions of political leaders. Keith Baker's *Inventing the French Revolution* (1990) took an approach that was more linguistic and philosophical than anthropological. Baker dissected the different "languages" or "discourses" in which political issues were discussed in France before and during the Revolution. He argued that the words in which revolutionary political debates were conducted defined and limited their possible outcomes. By de-emphasizing the importance of socioeconomic class in the Revolution, revisionist critics and cultural historians also opened the way for a new interest in the history of groups whose experience had previously been regarded as marginal. Joan Landes, in her *Women and the Public Sphere in the Age of the French Revolution* (1989), argued that the revolutionary movement was fundamentally antifeminist. Other scholars, however, including Lynn Hunt, Dominque Godineau, and Suzanne Desan, see the Revolution as providing important opportunities for women's political participation and broadening their civil rights, even though it also saw determined efforts to confine women to their "proper" domestic concerns. Whereas recent historians who concentrate on economic development have tended to see the social changes of the 1790s as less significant than those of the 1830s or 1840s, women's historians have suggested that the 1790s were indeed a defining decade in which new definitions of gender roles that persisted throughout the nineteenth century were established.

The celebration of the bicentennial of the French Revolution in 1989 took place at a moment when the revisionist and feminist critiques of the French Revolution had challenged long-established claims about the Revolution's contributions to the cause of democracy. In the 1990s, proponents of what can be called a neoliberal or neodemocratic interpretation of the Revolution reacted against these critiques. Isser Woloch's *The New Regime* (1993) showed that, for all its excesses, the Revolution had in fact successfully implemented more of its democratic program than the revisionists had been willing to acknowledge. John Markoff's *The Abolition of Feudalism* (1996) and Timothy Tackett's *Becoming a Revolutionary* (1996) both, in differing ways, reasserted the importance of economic interests and social class divisions in explaining revolutionary politics and countered the revisionists' tendency to portray the period's conflicts as purely ideological. Michel Biard's 2002 study of the Convention's "deputies on mission" proposed a more balanced understanding of the Terror period. In the years since 2000, scholarship has begun to temper these positive assessments of the Revolution with a renewed emphasis on the role of violence in the period's politics. Jean-Clément Martin's *Violence et Révolution*, Howard Brown's *Ending the French Revolution: Violence, Justice, and Repression from the Terror to Napoleon*, and Donald Sutherland's *Murder in Aubagne: Lynching, Law, and Justice during the French Revolution* are examples of this tendency. Marisa Linton's *Choosing Terror: Virtue, Friendship, and Authenticity in the French Revolution* emphasizes the fears that drove revolutionary leaders to turn on each other. A new interest in the Revolution's colonial dimension and the period's conflicts over slavery, highlighted in books by Laurent Dubois, Jeremy D. Popkin, and Philippe Girard, among others, has challenged the emphasis on the Revolution's contribution to modern ideas of liberty from another perspective.

The understanding that historians have of the French Revolution today is thus more nuanced and harder to sum up than it was a generation ago. Rather than a simple confrontation between past and future, feudalism and capitalism, or nobles and bourgeois, the events of the Revolution now seem to show us that the introduction of liberal and democratic principles was a complex and uneven process that undeniably exacted a high human cost. The revolutionaries made mistakes. They rejected compromises that might have reduced the antagonisms that wracked France after 1789, such as those caused by the attempt to reform the Church without taking devout Catholics' concerns into consideration. From a modern point of view, their treatment of women and the hesitations of their policy about slavery appear to be in flagrant contradiction with their own proclamations about universal human rights. Above all, the fact that the French Revolution not only turned to violent means to achieve its ends but that, for one brief but tragic period, it also made one-sided trials and public executions of its own supporters central to its policies must always be deeply troubling to those who sympathize with its ideals. Even as we recognize the French Revolution's failures and contradictions, however, it is impossible to exclude the movement that first proclaimed that "men are born and remain free and equal in rights," granted citizenship to religious minorities, voted to abolish slavery, and took so many initiatives to try to mitigate the effects of poverty and ignorance, from a central place in the development of modern notions of freedom and democracy.

Critical Thinking Questions

1. The Revolution and the Napoleonic period brought about major changes in French society. List the major transformations during this period. Consider whether they corresponded to the original goals of the revolutionaries of 1789.
2. Historians' assessments of the Revolution have continued to change throughout the course of the last two centuries. Describe the major changes in revolutionary historiography, from the early nineteenth century to the present. Why do historians continue to disagree about the significance of the Revolution?

Notes

1. Alfred de Musset, *La confession d'un enfant du siècle* (Paris: Gallimard, 1973), 26.
2. Cited in Steven Kaplan, *Farewell, Revolution* (Ithaca, NY: Cornell University Press, 1995), 137, 140.

APPENDIX

Chronology of Principal Events During the French Revolution

Prerevolutionary Crisis (January 1, 1787–May 5, 1789)

February 22, 1787: Assembly of Notables opens.

May 25, 1787: Assembly of Notables dissolved after refusing to accept reform proposals.

November 19, 1787: Compromise plan to solve fiscal crisis falls apart when Paris Parlement protests king's arbitrary order to accept it.

May 8, 1788: Royal ministers announce plan to abolish parlements and create new judicial system, setting off widespread protests.

July 5, 1788: Government announces convocation of Estates-General and suspends censorship.

July 13, 1788: Hailstorm damages crops in much of northern France, causing fears of famine.

August 26, 1788: Jacques Necker appointed as finance minister.

December 27, 1788: Royal Council announces "doubling of Third Estate," allowing commoners twice as many deputies as other estates in Estates-General.

January–April 1789: Convocation of electoral assemblies for Estates-General.

April 28, 1789: Reveillon riot in Paris shows extent of social tensions in capital.

May 5, 1789: Opening session of Estates-General.

The Liberal Revolution (May 5, 1789–August 10, 1792)

June 17, 1789: Deputies of Third Estate declare themselves the National Assembly.

June 20, 1789: National Assembly deputies swear Oath of the Tennis Court.

June 23, 1789: National Assembly defies Louis XVI's order for estates to meet separately.

June 27, 1789: Louis XVI orders deputies of clergy and nobility to join National Assembly.

July 11, 1789: Dismissal of Necker announced.

July 14, 1789: Paris crowd and soldiers storm the Bastille.

July 20–early August 1789: Wave of rural violence ("Great Fear") sweeps most of the country.

August 4–5, 1789: National Assembly decrees the abolition of seigneurial dues and special privileges.

August 26, 1789: National Assembly passes the "Declaration of the Rights of Man and Citizen."

September 11, 1789: National Assembly votes to give king suspensive rather than absolute veto.

October 5–6, 1789: Crowd of women and National Guard marches on Versailles and forces king and National Assembly to move to Paris.

November 2, 1789: National Assembly votes to expropriate Church lands.

July 12, 1790: Enactment of Church-reform plan, the Civil Constitution of the Clergy.

July 14, 1790: Festival of the Federation commemorates first anniversary of storming of Bastille.

May 15, 1791: Assembly votes to give political rights to some free people of color in colonies.

June 14, 1791: Le Chapelier law abolishes guilds and prohibits formation of trade unions.

June 20, 1791: Louis XVI and his family flee Paris. They are stopped at Varennes on June 22.

July 16, 1791: Paris Jacobin Club splits; supporters of the king form a new club, the Feuillants.

July 17, 1791: Paris National Guard kills sixty demonstrators in "massacre of Champ-de-Mars."

August 22, 1791: Beginning of slave insurrection in Saint-Domingue.

August 27, 1791: Austrian and Prussian rulers issue Pillnitz declaration, demanding restoration of Louis XVI's rights.

September 27, 1791: National Assembly votes to make all French Jews full citizens.

October 1, 1791: First session of the Legislative Assembly.

April 20, 1792: France declares war on Austria.

The Radical Revolution (August 10, 1792–July 27, 1794)

August 10, 1792: Sans-culotte militants attack royal palace, forcing Legislative Assembly to suspend king and call for election of National Convention.

September 2–5, 1792: "September massacres": Revolutionary activists kill suspected counterrevolutionaries in Paris prisons.

September 20, 1792: French victory at Valmy halts advance of the Austrian-Prussian army.

September 20, 1792: National Convention opens. On September 22, the Convention declares France a republic.

January 21, 1793: Execution of Louis XVI.

March 11, 1793: Vendée counterrevolutionary revolt breaks out.

May 31–June 2, 1793: Revolutionary activists force Convention to decree arrest of Girondins.

June 6, 1793: Start of federalist revolts against Convention.

July 13, 1793: Charlotte Corday assassinates Marat.

July 27, 1793: Robespierre elected to the Committee of Public Safety.

August 23, 1793: Convention decrees the "levée en masse."

September 5, 1793: Crowd urges Convention to declare that "terror is the order of the day"; general maximum on prices and wages.

September 17, 1793: Passage of Law of Suspects.

October 5, 1793: Convention establishes revolutionary calendar, prelude to radical phase of de-Christianization campaign in November 1793.

October 16, 1793: Execution of Marie-Antoinette.

October 31, 1793: Execution of twenty-one Girondin deputies .

December 4, 1793 (14 frimaire II): Convention puts all local officials under the authority of the Committee of Public Safety.

January 17, 1794: "Infernal columns" begin the bloodiest phase of the repression in the Vendée.

February 4, 1794 (16 pluviôse II): Convention abolishes slavery in French colonies.

February 26, 1794 (8 ventôse II): Convention votes for distribution of confiscated émigré property to poor patriots.

March 24, 1794 (4 germinal II): Revolutionary Tribunal condemns Hébert, the *Père Duchesne.*

April 6, 1794 (16 germinal II): Execution of "Indulgents" (Danton, Camille Desmoulins, and supporters).

June 8, 1794 (20 prairial II): Robespierre presides over Festival of the Supreme Being.

June 10, 1794 (22 prairial II): Law accelerating Revolutionary Tribunal's procedures marks start of "Great Terror."

June 26, 1794 (8 messidor II): French victory at Fleurus drives enemy armies out of France.

July 27, 1794 (9 thermidor II): Convention votes the arrest of Robespierre and his supporters.

The Thermidorian and Directory Periods (July 27, 1794–November 9, 1799)

April 1, 1795 (12 germinal II): Hunger crisis provokes sans-culottes to invade the Convention.

May 20–23, 1795 (1–4 prairial III): Final sans-culotte uprising; one Convention deputy is killed.

October 5, 1795 (13 vendémiaire IV): Defeat of counterrevolutionary uprising in Paris clears way for installation of new Directory regime.

May 10, 1796 (21 floréal IV): Arrest of Gracchus Babeuf and members of the "Conspiracy of the Equals."

September 4, 1797 (18 fructidor V): Coup d'état ousts counterrevolutionaries from Directory and legislature; start of "Second Directory."

October 17, 1797 (26 vendémiaire VI): Napoleon's treaty with Austria at Campo-Formio.

May 11, 1798 (22 floréal VI): Coup d'état prevents seating of neo-Jacobin deputies.

June 18, 1799 (30 prairial VII): Coup d'état ousts four members from Executive Directory.

November 9, 1799 (18 brumaire VIII): Directory overthrown by Sieyès and Napoleon.

The Napoleonic Period (November 9, 1799–June 18, 1815)

December 13, 1799: Napoleon Bonaparte made First Consul.

June 14, 1800: Napoleon's victory at Marengo consolidates his power in France.

February 9, 1801: Treaty of Lunéville between Austria and France.

July 16, 1801: Signature of Concordat between France and the Papacy, officially published on April 8, 1802.

March 25, 1802: Peace of Amiens between France and England.

May 19, 1802: Establishment of Legion of Honor.

May 20, 1802: Decree of 30 floréal X authorizes reintroduction of slavery in French colonies.

August 4, 1802: Napoleon becomes First Consul for Life.

March 28, 1803: War resumed between France and England.

November 18, 1803: French troops surrender to black insurgents in Saint-Domingue, which becomes the independent nation of Haiti on January 1, 1804.

March 20, 1804: Execution of duc d'Enghien.

March 21, 1804: Proclamation of the Civil Code (Code Napoleon).

December 2, 1804: Napoleon crowns himself as Emperor, with Pope in attendance.

December 2, 1805: Battle of Austerlitz.

October 14, 1806: Battles of Jena and Auerstädt shatter Prussian army.

November 21, 1806: Napoleon declares Continental Blockade against trade with Britain.

July 7, 1807: Treaty of Tilsit with Russia.

March 1, 1808: Napoleon announces creation of new system of nobility.

May 1808: Anti-French uprising in Madrid leads to reprisals that fan Spanish resistance.

June 11, 1809: Pope Pius VII excommunicates Napoleon.

July 5–6, 1809: Battle of Wagram.

April 2, 1810: After divorcing Josephine, Napoleon marries the Austrian princess Marie-Louise.

June 1812: Napoleon starts invasion of Russia. Forced into disastrous retreat in late October, he loses most of his army.

October 16–19, 1813: "Battle of the Nations" at Leipzig opens way for invasion of France.

April 6, 1814: Napoleon abdicates as Emperor.

March 20, 1815: After landing in southern France on March 1, Napoleon arrives in Paris and inaugurates the "Hundred Days."

June 18, 1815: Allied forces under the command of Wellington defeat the French at Waterloo.

SUGGESTIONS FOR FURTHER READING

This short bibliography is meant to direct students to reference works that will help them find more specialized readings, to some of the more general books in the field, and to a selection of specialized monographs of particular interest. With a few exceptions, it is limited to titles available in English. References to relevant works in French can be found in the bibliographies of most of the books listed here.

Journals and Reference Works

Many scholarly journals in English publish articles on the revolutionary and Napoleonic periods, including *French Historical Studies, French History,* and the *Journal of Modern History.* The French journal *Annales historiques de la Révolution française* is devoted entirely to the subject. The online service *H-France.net* is a forum for reviews of new books and discussion of scholarly issues.

Useful reference works include Paul Hanson, *Historical Dictionary of the French Revolution* (2004); Samuel Scott and Barry Rothaus, eds., *Historical Dictionary of the French Revolution* (1985); and Owen Connelly, ed., *Historical Dictionary of Napoleonic France* (1985). François Furet and Mona Ozouf, eds., *Critical Dictionary of the French Revolution* (1989) includes longer interpretive articles reflecting the revisionist perspective on the Revolution.

Specialized Titles: Select Bibliography

General Histories and Document Collections

Simon Schama's *Citizens* (1989) is a dramatic narrative history, rather one-sided in its stress on the Revolution's violence. William Doyle, *Oxford History of the French Revolution* (2nd ed., 2003) is a detailed political account extending through 1802; Donald Sutherland, *French Revolution and Empire* (2003) gives greater attention to social history and covers the entire Napoleonic period. Alan Forrest, *The French Revolution* (1995) is a concise overview organized on thematic, rather than chronological, lines. An older work still worth consulting is the synthesis by the leading French historian of the twentieth century, Georges Lefebvre, *The French Revolution,* 2 vols. (1962). Useful collections of translated documents include Paul Beik, *The French Revolution* (1970); J. H. Stewart, *Documentary Survey of the French Revolution* (1951); and Laura Mason and Tracey Rizzo, *The French Revolution: A Document Collection* (1999). Lynn Hunt and Jack Censer, *Liberty, Equality, Fraternity* (2001), a collection of documents and images from the period, is accessible online through the website of the Center for History and New Media, *chnm.gmu.edu/revolution.* Lynn Hunt, ed., *The French Revolution and Human Rights* (1996) gives the main speeches from revolutionary debates on this issue. Laurent Dubois and John Garrigus, eds., *Slave Revolution in the Caribbean* (2006) and David Geggus, *The Haitian Revolution: A Documentary History* (2014) are collections of documents about the struggle against slavery in the French colonies. Frank Kafker and James Laux, *The French Revolution: Conflicting Interpretations* (1990) provides excerpts from many older historical works. Steven Kaplan, *Farewell, Revolution* (1995) is a detailed account of how France marked the 200th anniversary of the Revolution in 1989.

The Old Regime and the Origins of the Revolution

A classic interpretation of the connection between the Old Regime and the Revolution, still valuable for its many brilliant insights, is Alexis de Tocqueville, *The Old Regime and the Revolution* (1955; orig. 1856). Roger Chartier, *Cultural Origins of the French Revolution* (1991) and Daniel Roche, *France in the Enlightenment* (1998) outline the changes in French culture and society that made the Revolution possible. Robert Darnton, *The Forbidden Best-Sellers of Pre-Revolutionary France* (1995) looks at the circulation of subversive texts. The development of an independent public opinion is a major theme in Thomas Crow, *Painters and Public Life in Eighteenth-Century France* (1985). Sarah Maza, *Private Lives and Public Affairs* (1993) studies how prerevolutionary scandals undermined the regime, and Carolyn Weber, *Queen of Fashion: What Marie Antoinette Wore to the Revolution* (2006) looks at the Queen's role from an original angle. David Bell, *The Cult of the Nation* (2001) and John Shovlin, *The Political Economy of Virtue: Luxury, Patriotism and the Origins of the French Revolution* (2006) trace the development of key revolutionary concepts. Dan Edelstein, *The Terror of Natural Right* (2009) argues that Enlightenment thought concealed the germs of revolutionary political intolerance.

Dale Van Kley has summarized his extensive research on the influence of Jansenism in *The Religious Origins of the French Revolution* (1996). The impact of the political crisis resulting from Louis XV's final attempt to silence the parlementary opposition is the subject of many of the essays in Keith Baker, *Inventing the French Revolution* (1990). Michael Kwass, *Privilege and the Politics of Taxation in Eighteenth-Century France* (2000) shows the impact of prerevolutionary debates about finances. Munro Price, *Preserving the Monarchy: The Comte de Vergennes* (1995) traces French foreign policy in the era of the American Revolution. Jean Egret, *The French Prerevolution* (1977) remains the standard account of the political events of 1787 and 1788. Georges Lefebvre's *Coming of the French Revolution* (1947) was for decades the authoritative work on the subject. William Doyle's *Origins of the French Revolution,* 3rd ed. (1999), offers an updated analysis. Peter Campbell, ed., *The Origins of the French Revolution* (2006), and Thomas Kaiser and Dale Van Kley, eds., *From Deficit to Deluge* (2011) are recent collections of essays on the causes of the Revolution.

Revolutionary Politics

Timothy Tackett, *Becoming a Revolutionary: The Deputies of the French National Assembly and the Emergence of a Revolutionary Culture* (1996) studies the politics of the Revolution's first assembly, and the same author's *When the King Took Flight* (2003) recounts the Varennes crisis. Timothy Tackett, *Religion, Revolution, and Regional Culture in Eighteenth-Century France* (1986) and Suzanne Desan, *Reclaiming the Sacred* (1990) examine the social bases underlying the religious conflict, whose stages are recounted in Nigel Aston, *Religion and Revolution in France* (2000). Alan Forrest, *Paris, the Provinces and the French Revolution* (2004), and Paul Hanson, *The Jacobin Republic under Fire* (2003) look at the tensions between Paris and the provinces. Isser Woloch, *The New Regime* (1993) provides a comprehensive overview at the movement's impact on civic institutions.

Marisa Linton's *Choosing Terror: Virtue, Friendship, and Authenticity in the French Revolution* (2013) provides a fresh look at the dramatic interactions between revolutionary leaders, a subject also central to Charles Walton's *Policing Public Opinion in the French Revolution* (2009). The essays in Peter Campbell, Thomas Kaiser, and Marisa Linton, eds., *Conspiracy in the French Revolution* (2010) explore a central feature of the revolutionary political mentality. The multivocal approach of Norman Hampson, *Life and Opinions of Maximilien Robespierre* (1974) emphasizes the conflicting interpretations that have been offered of the most controversial revolutionary leader; more recent biographies of the "Incorruptible" include David Jordan, *The Revolutionary Career of Maximilien Robespierre* (1985), and Peter McPhee, *Robespierre: A Revolutionary Life* (2012). R. R. Palmer's classic *Twelve Who Ruled* (1943) explains the Committee of Public Safety's policies; David Andress, *The Terror* (2006) looks at the Terror more broadly. Alyssa Sepinwall, *The Abbé Grégoire and the French Revolution* (2005) treats the career of one of the movement's great champions of human rights, and Siân Reynolds, *Marriage and Revolution: Monsieur and Madame Roland* (2012) meshes the story of the Revolution's most famous woman politician with that of her influential husband. R. B. Rose, *Gracchus Babeuf* (1978) looks at one of the most radical revolutionary thinkers, whereas Darrin McMahon, *Enemies of the Enlightenment* (2001) discusses conservative critics of the Revolution. David P. Jordan's *The King's Trial* (1979) vividly describes one of the Revolution's turning points; speeches from the trial are translated in Michael Walzer, ed., *Regicide and Revolution* (1992), while John Hardman, *Louis XVI* (1993) gives a sympathetic portrait of the king. T. C. W. Blanning, *Origins of the French Revolutionary Wars* (1986) explains international aspects of the revolutionary conflict.

Revolutionary Culture

François Furet's essay *Interpreting the French Revolution* (1981) opened a new era of historiography, focused on the Revolution's political culture. Lynn Hunt, *Politics, Culture and Class in the French Revolution* (1984) and Mona Ozouf, *Festivals and the French Revolution* (1988) offer stimulating explorations of this subject. Jeremy Popkin, *Revolutionary News* (1990) deals with the newspaper press, and Emmet Kennedy, *Cultural History of the French Revolution* (1989) covers the entire range of cultural activities. Laura Mason, *Singing the French Revolution* (1996) describes popular revolutionary music, and H.-J. Lüsebrink and Rolf Reichardt, *The Bastille: A History of a Symbol of Despotism and Freedom* (1997) looks at the development of the most potent symbol of the Revolution. Antoine de Baecque, *Glory and Terror: Seven Deaths under the French Revolution* (2001) uses the deaths of prominent figures to explore the changing atmosphere of the Revolution. Charles Gillispie, *Science and Polity in France: The Revolutionary and Napoleonic Years* (2004) argues that the era saw fundamental changes in science.

Social and Women's History

With the dissolution of the Marxist paradigm, there is no convincing synthesis of the complex social history of the revolutionary period. Peter Jones, *The Peasantry in the French Revolution* (1988) gives an overview of the revolution in the countryside, and his *Liberty and Locality in Revolutionary France* (2003) offers a readable account of institutional change at the village level. Charles Tilly, *The Vendée* (1967) used the counterrevolutionary peasant revolt to build an influential general model explaining social protest. John Markoff, *The Abolition of Feudalism* (1996) is a major reexamination of the peasantry's role in the Revolution. The urban revolutionary movement is the subject of Albert Soboul, *The Sans-Culottes* (1964); George Rudé, *The Crowd in the French Revolution* (1959); and Richard Cobb, *The Police and the People* (1970). On women during the Revolution, see the documentary collection, Darline Gay Levy et al., *Women in Revolutionary Paris* (1979); the interpretation of the Revolution as an anti-feminist movement put forward by Joan Landes, *Women and the Public Sphere in the Age of the French Revolution* (1989); Sara Melzer and Leslie Rabine, eds., *Rebel Daughters: Women and the French Revolution* (1992); Olwyn Hufton, *Women and the Limits of Citizenship in the French Revolution* (1992); and Dominique Godineau, *The Women of Paris and Their French Revolution* (1998). Suzanne Desan, *The Family on Trial in Revolutionary France* (2004) argues that the Revolution's egalitarian legislation was overturned in the Napoleonic period, and Jennifer Heuer, *The Family and the Nation* (2005) shows how changing definitions of citizenship affected women. Alan Forrest has examined two important groups in the revolutionary period in his *The French Revolution and the Poor* (1981) and

Soldiers of the French Revolution (1990). Dora Weiner's *The Citizen-Patient in Revolutionary and Imperial Paris* (1993) looks at the Revolution's impact on medical treatment.

On the revolution in Saint-Domingue, the classic account in C. L. R. James, *The Black Jacobins* (1963) has been superseded by more recent scholarship, notably Laurent Dubois, *Avengers of the New World* (2004), and Jeremy D. Popkin, *Concise History of the Haitian Revolution* (2012). John Garrigus, *Before Haiti: Race and Citizenship in French Saint-Domingue* (2006) examines the role of the colony's free people of color in the revolutionary era, and Jeremy D. Popkin, *You Are All Free: The Haitian Revolution and the Abolition of Slavery* (2010) traces the events on both sides of the Atlantic that led to 1794 decree abolishing slavery. Laurent Dubois, *A Colony of Citizens* (2004) treats Guadeloupe, another major French colony. Two recent collections of essays on the global dimensions of the Revolution's impact are David Armitage and Sanjay Subrahmanyam, *The Age of Revolutions in Global Context* (2010) and Suzanne Desan, Lynn Hunt, and William Max Nelson, eds., *The French Revolution in Global Perspective* (2013).

Directory Period

James Livesey's controversial *Making Democracy in the French Revolution* (2001) drew new attention to this period by claiming that the regime should be credited with laying the bases for French democracy, whereas Howard Brown, *Ending the French Revolution: Violence, Justice, and Repression from the Terror to Napoleon* (2006) argues that it foreshadowed Napoleon's police state and Andrew Jainchill, *Reimagining Politics after the Terror* (2008) sees the period as the seedtime of France's tradition of elitist liberalism. Bronislaw Baczko, *Ending the Terror* (1994) explains how the thermidorians tried to deal with the legacy of 1794. Martyn Lyons, *France under the Directory* (1975) is a useful overview; Isser Woloch, *Jacobin Legacy* (1970) looks at the period's left-wing movement, whereas Harvey Mitchell, *The Underground War against Revolutionary France* (1965) and Jeremy D. Popkin, *The Right-Wing Press in France, 1792–1800* (1980) treat counterrevolutionary opposition to the Republic. R. R. Palmer, *The World of the French Revolution* (1971) provides a brief account of the "sister republics." Juan Cole, *Napoleon's Egypt: Invading the Middle East* (2007) explores Arab reactions to Napoleon's expedition.

Napoleonic Period

Most of the literature on this period focuses on Napoleon, rather than on France. A major exception is Louis Bergeron's *France under Napoleon* (1981), which emphasizes the experience of the French people rather than Napoleon's life. Philip Dwyer's two volumes *Napoleon: The Path to Power* (2008) and *Citizen Emperor: Napoleon in Power* (2013) offer the most recent scholarly biography in English of the most celebrated Frenchman of all times. The same author's *Napoleon and Europe* (2001) is a useful collection of essays. J. C. Herold, *The Mind of Napoleon* (1955) and Rafe Blaufarb, *Napoleon: A Symbol for an Age* (2007) include translated documents about the period. Robert Holtman, *Napoleonic Propaganda* (1950) and Isser Woloch, *Napoleon and His Collaborators* (2001) discuss domestic aspects of the reign. Charles Esdaile, *Napoleon's Wars* (2007) covers the period's military conflicts. Geoffrey Ellis, *Napoleon's Continental Blockade* (1981) studies the effects of Napoleon's economic warfare. Alan Forrest, *Napoleon's Men: The Soldiers of the Revolution and Empire* (2002) and David A. Bell, *The First Total War: Napoleon's Europe and the Birth of Warfare as We Know It* (2007) discuss the period's "war culture." Philippe Girard, *The Slaves Who Defeated Napoleon* (2011) tells the story of Napoleon's brutal effort to restore white rule in France's most important colony.

CREDITS

Text Credits

Chapter 1:

Pg. 2, Cited in the University of Chicago College History Staff, eds., History of Western Civilization (Chicago: University of Chicago Press, 1977), 57; pg. 2, Translation by Jeremy D. Popkin; pg. 7, Alexis de Tocqueville, The Old Regime and the French Revolution (New York: Doubleday, 1955), 177; pg. 12, Jacques Ménétra, Journal of My Life, trans. Arthur Goldhammer (New York: Columbia University Press, 1986), 171; pg.12–13, John Lough, France on the Eve of Revolution (Chicago: Dorsey, 1987), 34, 45.

Chapter 2:

Pg. 20, Cited in Jean Egret, The French Pre-Revolution, 1787–1788, Wesley D. Camp, trans. (Chicago: University of Chicago Press, 1977), 2; pg. 21, Charles Alexandre de Calonne; pg. 21, King Louis XIV, before the Parlement de Paris, 1655, translation appears in Doyle, W. Origins of the French Revolution. Oxford University Press, 1980; pg. 23, Sieyès, cited in John Hall Stewart, A Documentary Survey of the French Revolution (New York: Macmillan, 1951), 42–44; pg. 24, From Rabaut Saint-Etienne, Considerations sur les intérêts du Tiers-Etat [1788] pp. 35–37. Translation by Jeremy D. Popkin; pg. 27, Count Mirabeau. Translation by Jeremy D. Popkin; pg. 29, J. B. Dusaulx, L'Oeuvre de sept jours [Paris, 1790]. Translation by Jeremy D. Popkin; pg. 29, From Révolutions de Paris, no. 1 [12–19 July 1789]. Translation by Jeremy D. Popkin; pg. 29, From Gazette de Leyde, 31 July 1789. Translation by Jeremy D. Popkin; pg. 30, Cited in J. M. Roberts, ed., French Revolution Documents (Oxford: Basil Blackwell, 1966), 141.

Chapter 3:

Pg. 31, Révolutions de Paris, July 1789; pg. 38, Cited in Guy Chaussinand-Nogaret, Mirabeau (Paris: Seuil, 1982), 224; pg. 40, Cited in George Rudé, ed., Robespierre (Upper Saddle River, N.J.: Prentice Hall, 1967), 14; pg. 41, Cited in Florin Aftalion, L'économie de la Révolution française (Paris: Hachette, 1987), 91.

Chapter 4:

Pg. 49, Journal général de la cour et de la ville, 28 June 1791; pg. 49, Gazette universelle, 10 July 1791; pg. 49, L'Ami du peuple, 15 July 1791) (Translations by Jeremy D. Popkin.); pg. 50, Edmund Burke, an English observer, February 1790; pg. 50, Joel Barlow, American poet, 1791; pg. 50, Cited in Esther E. Brown, The French Revolution and the American Man of Letters (Columbia, Mo., 1951), 82, 91; pg. 53, Translation by Jeremy D. Popkin; pg. 59, Georges Danton.

Chapter 5:

Pg. 64, Cited in David Jordan, The King's Trial (Berkeley: University of California Press, 1979), 136, 172; pg. 64, Saint-Just, Oeuvres choisies (Paris: Gallimard, 1968), 76; pg. 68, Cited in William Sewell, Work and Revolution in France [Cambridge: Cambridge University Press, 1980] p. 110; pg. 68, From Buchez and Roux, Histoire parlementaire, vol. 28, pp. 216–217. Translation by Jeremy D. Popkin; pg. 71, Translated by Jeremy D. Popkin from Gazette Universelle; pg. 72, Translated by Jeremy D. Popkin from Ami du Peuple; pg. 72, Cited in Louis Trénard, Lyon de l'Encyclopédie au préromantisme (Paris: Presses Universitaires de France, 1958), 365; pg. 73, Cited in Serge Bianchi, La révolution culturelle de l'an II (Paris: Aubier, 1982), 197; pg. 74, sans-culotte leader Chaumette, translated in The French Revolution and Human Rights: A Brief Documentary History, translated, edited, and with an introduction by Lynn Hunt (Bedford/St. Martin's: Boston/New York), 1996, 138–39; pg. 75, From Journal de la Montagne, 23 plu. II. Translation by Jeremy D. Popkin; pg. 75, Vergniaud, 1793, translated by Thomas Carlyle, The French Revolution, Chapman and Hall, 1837; pg. 76, Saint-Just, translated in "The French Revolution," by George Rude, Grove Press, 1991; pg. 78, Jean François Noel, L'Ombre et la lumière: Mémoires d'un bourgeois de Dombes. (Translated by Jeremy D. Popkin.).

Chapter 6:

Pg. 89, François Pairault, Gaspard Monge, le fondateur de Polytechnique (Paris: Taillander, 2000), 373; Napoleon in Egypt: Al-Jabarti's Chronicle of the French Occupation, 1798, trans. Shmuel Moreh (Princeton, N.J.: Markus Weiner Publishing, 1975), 93; pg. 90, Ami des lois, 20 prairial An VI (7 June 1798). Translated by Jeremy D. Popkin.

Chapter 7:

Pg. 100, Leclerc, letter to Napoleon, 7 Oct. 1802, in Paul Roussier, ed., Lettres du Général Leclerc (Paris: Société pour l'histoire des colonies françaises, 1937), 256; pg. 101, Cited in J. Christopher Herold, The Mind of Napoleon (New York: Columbia University Press, 1955), 104; pg. 102, Cited in Felix Markham, Napoleon (New York: Mentor, 1963), 95; pg. 103, L'Ange Gabriel, 21 niv. VIII.

Chapter 8:

Pg. 106, From Count Las Cases, Life of Napoleon [1835]; pg. 106, Talleyrand, Napoleon's foreign minister; pg. 107, Cited in Felix Markham, Napoleon (New York: Mentor, 1963), 113; pg. 111, Cited in Rafe Blaufard, Napoleon: Symbol for an Age (Boston: Bedford, 2008), 96; pg. 112, From F. Guizot, Mémoires pour servir à l'histoire de mon temps [Paris: Michel Lévy fréres,1858] vol. 1, pp. 7, 13. Translation by Jeremy D. Popkin; pg. 113, Cited in J. Christopher Herold, The Mind of Napoleon (New York: Columbia University Press, 1955), 18; pg. 115, Cited in James Woodness, A Yankee's Odyssey: The Life of Joel Barlow (Philadelphia: Lippincott, 1958), 277.

Chapter 9:

Pg. 119, Alfred de Musset, La confession d'un enfant du siècle (Paris: Gallimard, 1973), 26; pg. 121, Cited in Steven Kaplan, Farewell, Revolution (Ithaca, N.Y.: Cornell University Press, 1995), 137, 140.

Photo Credits

Chapter 1:

Pg. 3, The British Library Board.

Chapter 2:

Pg. 28, Library of Congress Prints and Photographs Division Washington, D.C. 20540 USA http://hdl.loc.gov/loc.pnp/pp.print.

Chapter 3:

Pg. 34, Photos 12/Alamy.

Chapter 4:

Pg. 52, Réunion des Musées Nationaux/Art Resource, NY; pg. 60, Scala/White Images/Art Resource, NY.

Chapter 5:

Pg. 63, Library of Congress Prints and Photographs Division Washington, D.C. 20540 USA; pg. 77, Library of Congress Prints and Photographs Division Washington, D.C. 20540 USA http://hdl.loc.gov/loc.pnp/pp.print.

Chapter 6:

Pg. 89, Huntington Library/SuperStock.

Chapter 7:

Pg. 95, Library of Congress (b&w film copy neg.) cph 3b43113 http://hdl.loc.gov/loc.pnp/cph.3b43113.

Chapter 8:

Pg. 107, Library of Congress Prints and Photographs Division Washington, D.C. 20540 USA.COVER: Scala/White Images/Art Resource, NY.

INDEX